God won't vote
this year

God won't vote
this year

DAVID ZANOTTI

First published in 2007 by
THE AMERICAN POLICY ROUNDTABLE
National Headquarters
11288 Alameda Drive
Strongsville, Ohio 44149

For more information about the American Policy Roundtable
log on to www.APRoundtable.org.

ISBN: 0-9779632-1-7

Unless otherwise indicated, Bible quotations are taken from The New International Version of the Bible. Copyright (c) 1978 by the International Bible Society.

TABLE OF CONTENTS

Introduction

Baseball is called America's national pastime. Some would argue it is football. Some will argue over just about anything. History might well prove the real pastime of Americans has always been politics. Sooner or later every American feels a sense of investment in something political. For some it is a casual obligation. For others it is a blood sport.

In the 1950's and 60's, good mothers taught their children to not talk about politics or religion in public. By the 1970's those same children took the anti-war movement to the front of Time magazine. This book is not a text those dear moms of the 50's would likely recommend.

This book is written to Americans and for Americans who want to do "the right thing" when it comes to politics but may not always be certain what "the right thing" is. Those who feel they have all the answers figured out will find this book most aggravating.

The stuff of politics is tricky. Politics can be as mundane as a traffic light or as life-threatening as a speeding car running a red light. This brief work is designed for those looking for genuine answers on voting and citizenship but who won't want to get run over in the process.

Every election cycle, millions of Americans go to the polls to decide who catches dogs and settles zoning arguments. Those same voters determine the make up of the entire judicial system and the direction of American foreign policy across the globe.

Yet, only about 50% of the people who could engage in the process of voting actually participate. It has been that way for a long, long time. The blessings of Liberty, including the hard-earned right to vote, are often left on the shelf by contemporary Americans.

Should we feel guilty about not voting? Why bother when there is so little evidence that my single vote will even matter? How does standing in line on a cold November day and casting a single ballot add up to changing the state and nation?

In the following pages evidence will be presented in the hope of answering these questions. Words will be kept to an absolute minimum as the goal of this work is both clarity and brevity. Hopefully in the time it takes to fly from one city to the next or watch a few TV shows or a ball game (with one eye on the replays) this text can be added to the mental inventory.

Time for an important disclaimer: the author is a political independent, not affiliated with any political party or candidate, nor beholden to any political parties or media elites. The information presented here comes from thirty years of full-contact involvement in the political process across many states, from the local school board level to the White House. The analysis offered is based on real life experience in the arena, not something read in a textbook or on the Internet.

While I would love to write this work with the anonymity of Lemony Snicket, the media will not permit it. For those discovering the work of the American Policy Roundtable for the first time, or who are curious about how we have survived a lifetime on the mission field of American public policy, a full biography is presented in the appendix. You can also learn much more by visiting The Public Square®, our daily radio meeting place, at APRoundtable.org.

I wish I could name names in this text to provide storied examples of so many lessons learned in public life. That book remains to be written. For now, it is time to begin solving the current puzzle.

Chapter One
America – We Have a Problem

We don't like to talk about it much. It's a family problem that we keep hoping will go away. Maybe, if we give it enough time, it will get better. But it's not getting better and we have to face it every few years.

The way we do elections in this country is not working very well, especially at the top of the political pyramid. Approval ratings for the US Congress are awful, yet every two years the vast majority of House members run virtually unopposed and are re-elected. Un-electing an incumbent US Senator is about as easy as winning a TV reality show. How can this be in a land founded on the principle of limited, representative government?

We live in a country dominated by choices. Our grocery stores are filled with endless selections. The pen, pencil and marker section in the office supply store gives us thousands of instruments to write and color our words. Digital communications provide endless options to read, view, copy and send more radio, TV, video and print materials than in the history of the world. Yet every four years, we get to pick between two or perhaps three candidates for the Presidency of the United States.

The problem presents long term and short term challenges

to every voting citizen. One long term problem is the failure of political parties to adapt to the digital world. Political parties are virtually irrelevant to the common American life. At the same time, political party leaders have worked the system of state and federal election laws, including redistricting, so that it is extremely difficult for new political parties or candidate to gain ballot access and full recognition.

So every election cycle, "we the people" are presented with limited choices for leaders who must face an unlimited number of political and legal challenges on our behalf. This is the long-term problem.

In the short run, another election is coming and Americans have to pick between two or maybe three candidates running for the White House. People who want to do the right thing, who want to match their vote with a candidate that will represent them, are having a terrible time with the process. Imagine a room full of children and a single flannel graph board (for those under 30, flannel graphs are non-digital smart boards) in the front of the room. On the flannel graph are two or three stick figures. Each child is given a chance to place something on the board—to "dress-up" the stick figures in a way that best represents what they believe. At the end of the process, there are a lot of frustrated kids and a pretty meaningless, messy board. There simply is not enough room to express all of these opinions on the flannel graph.

The original American political design is wonderful, especially in the light of historical comparison. But the American political process is far from perfect. It provides choices, but limited choices. It is designed to be a representative form of government, but the people have to fight way too hard to get heard in the process. There are problems on both sides of the equation. The elected politicians at the state and federal level have become a mandarin class in American life. They are secluded, iconoclastic, arrogant and mostly out of touch with the realities of everyday life. Not all of them, but many of them, are downright hostile to "Joe Lunch Bucket" and his family. Yes, politicians talk about people in those terms, every single day.

Joe and Sallie Lunch Bucket, on the other hand, have largely checked out of the basic responsibility of holding elected officials accountable. They are so busy paying their taxes (thanks to the politicians) and chasing the American Dream that they barely have time to function as a family. Politics takes a seat way in the back of the bus.

The less we the people participate in government, the more the political class prospers. Government is big, big business in America today; in fact, it is the biggest business in America. If voters, who are the true shareholders, don't show up for regular board meetings and annual elections, then the politicians will make all the decisions. They do just that everyday and they send the shareholders the bill.

So what's the average voter to do? First we have to admit we have problems. The denial has to stop. We need a massive national intervention on behalf of the core principles of our Constitutional government. A revival of the Founding Spirit, a repentance for our lack of care and commitment, a long conversation and action plan on how to improve the political process to forward more leaders, better leaders, and braver leaders. This must start today and continue for however long it takes to fix the problems.

In the short term, we have to figure out who to vote for in the upcoming election. The process problems won't get fixed in one election cycle so we have to fight the temptation to walk away from the electoral process altogether. That kind of protesting feels good for a while, but it only empowers the elitists to take more ground.

We have to figure out who to vote for in the short term, while we stay committed to fixing the process in the long term. That's the grown up way to deal with the challenge. We could go the other way. We could simply throw up our hands in protest and walk away from voting altogether. "Let the idiots fend for themselves," some charge. "Sure the country will suffer, the economy will be hurt, basic civil liberties will be at risk – but too bad. Enough is enough. Let the system fall. The more pain, the faster real reform will take place."

There are some who will make this argument and claim it is the moral high ground. The faster the existing system falls, the faster we can get on with re-assembling America along the intentions of the original constitutional design. Unfortunately, those who advocate this "protest" position the loudest are not fighting to be the first in line to suffer the consequences of the total collapse they advocate.

Restoring truly constitutional, representative government is America's greatest political challenge. It is an internal infrastructure problem. It requires citizen participation at the voting booth and in the halls of the Statehouse and Congress. Protest is certainly part of the process, but great nations are not built solely by protest. The longer term work of reform will take a generation. It all begins with showing up at the polls and voting.

"But what if I despise the candidates at the top of the ticket?" Find the best choice, make no choice, skip the race and start voting down the ballot. "Is that legal?" Yes it is legal. No one is required to vote every race on the ballot. What is truly important is that people stay connected to the process in the short term and fight the battle for reform in the long term.

"But I'm tired, overworked, over-taxed and just don't have the time, energy, money, desire (pick one) to stick with this problem. I'm an American and I don't have to put up with this!"

No, you're an American — constitutional government is your birthright and responsibility — so deal with it. Whiners are supposed to live somewhere other than the land of the free and the home of the brave. Here in America things are very different from other places and other times. The people who designed America believed the Creator gave certain fundamental rights to mankind. They began the Constitution with the words "We the People" for a very specific reason. They believed that the authority to establish a government, write laws and enforce them resides first and foremost with "We the people." Those we elect to serve in our system of government are just that: "public servants." They are worthy of respect, honor and certainly an honest wage, but they are not above the law, nor are they above the political authority that ultimately resides in a concept known as the consent of the governed.

The problem we have in America is not in the original design or core principles. The solution begins with discovering what we have forgotten.

Chapter Two
The Perfect or Nothing

"He's more conservative."

"She is better qualified."

"Neither of them have the name ID or money to win the election."

"I'll never vote for her because she is soft on abortion and permits exceptions."

"I'll never support him because he used to be pro-abortion and flipped ten years ago."

"Yeah, but he raised taxes back in '98 and I can't forget that."

"But she has never taken a strong stand on school choice or the 2nd Amendment."

On and on the political squabbling goes. It ends up sounding like the sound track from one of those old barnyard cartoons from the 1940's with hens and roosters all fighting for control of the chicken coop. Every now and then this "political" game breaks out onto cable TV or talk radio in a full-fledged shouting match. Welcome inside the world of political activism, consulting and campaigns. Any wonder why common sense Americans turn the channel and go back to sitcoms, soap operas and ball games?

A lot of what happens in politics is dumb. Honest citizens try to stay away from the toxic waste dump of partisan politics the same way they duck out early on Thanksgiving dinner when the "stupid" in-law shows up. Americans smell phony, agenda driven politics even before they see it and try to steer clear at all costs.

But civil government is important. Just watch how "politically concerned" people become when basements start flooding or garbage is not picked-up, or a problem arises at the local high school, or a terrorist attack hits American soil.

We may not like it, we may try to avoid it, even compartmentalize it to a once-a-year or once-every-four-year reality, but Americans have to do electoral politics because it matters – a lot. Like solving a jigsaw puzzle, we have to pick between people and issues every election season. How we do the sorting becomes the stuff of legend in political and media circles. Here is a look behind the scenes on how the real system works.

Creating the "right" candidate

There are not a lot of business cards that read "Bill Jones – full-time political candidate." People who are running for office, especially high political office, are almost always gainfully employed doing some big work of service or industry. Usually if they are running for President, they are a member of Congress, a Governor, or a former high office holder. They all think they could be President someday, but they are very busy people, too busy to get to the White House without help. Few have the time to sit around plotting how they can win 51% of the Electoral College vote and become President of the United States. (Cue the theme music for the political consultants and gurus right here.)

So how does this very busy office holder or celebrity move

from Presidential wannabe to a real candidate? The first step is name recognition. To be elected, a person first has to be known by the general public. There is a group of full time professionals in America known as political consultants, who make a very good living helping wannabes turn into candidates. These consultants are joined at the hip with professional polling companies. Together they are constantly polling public opinion and watching the 24 hour news cycle. They are looking for names that begin to show up favorably in the minds of "the people."

When the former Mayor of BigTown or Governor of Massarkansia or Senator Wonderhair starts showing up favorably in the opinion polls, an amazing mating season begins. The political consultants and the wannabe candidates start looking for each other. The politician-celebrity figure scans the field of qualified, experienced political consulting firms, polling agencies, and media producers. The union of the candidate and the consultants is an intertwining of objectives and expectations. The candidate wants to win. The consultant wants to get paid big bucks out of the campaign war chest. To win, the candidate must get 50.1% of the vote and in Presidential races, 270 electoral votes. To get paid, the consultant has to make the candidate believe the campaign will succeed. Note: Consultants get paid before Election Day. They learned long ago that consulting is not a "commission-based" industry. They get paid if their candidate succeeds or fails.

Do ideology and issues come into play in this political mating process? Not as much as people might think. Sure, a die-hard Republican firm won't take on a life-time Democrat client (most of the time). But getting elected in the modern era is not about getting people to accept the candidate's platform. It's about getting 50.1%

of the people to vote for the candidate. If issues help get the vote, then fine. If pretty hair and pedigree are sufficient to win the day – that works as well. Candidates and consultants understand there is a huge difference between getting elected and governing. The former is how everyone gets paid. The latter is what the candidate is obligated to do afterwards.

When the candidate for national office appears and the union is complete, the first offspring is usually a campaign strategy document. For insiders this is the "**playbook**," not unlike the playbook for an NFL team. The early editions of the candidate playbook are dominated by "benchmark" polling data which shows where the candidate is starting the race. Progress (and sometimes paychecks) are marked from these starting polls.

A second key battery of polls determine what issues will dominate the race and tests voter approval on positions the candidate may or may not take on these key issues. Here the puzzle gets most complicated and intriguing. Pollsters bill campaigns millions of dollars annually, tearing apart issues and language and testing opinions on voters by telephone surveys and actual focus groups. A **focus group** is a group of people who sit in a small room being observed either from two way mirrors or video cameras. The group discusses a series of issues "facilitated" by a staff member of the polling company. The results of the focus group discussions are parsed, sub-divided, and rehashed, then all the data is reassembled into conclusions which are then presented to the candidate. Then the team sits down and decides what the candidate and the campaign have to do to create **a universe of voters** that will assure a victory on Election Day.

When the conversation turns to issues, the consultants pitch goes: *"Here are the polling results on key issues in this race. Seventy percent of the people favor term limits. We have to get those votes. Oh, the candidate is opposed to term limits? Not a problem. Place term limits in the 'negatives' column and begin the research and creative writing to 'nuance' the candidate's position on term limits so we don't lose voters on that issue."*

"62% of the voters favor elimination of the Inheritance Tax? Where are we on that one? The candidate loves that issue and her record is clear. Excellent, move Inheritance Tax Reform up in the offensive side of the playbook."

Pick an issue from A to Z - start with Abortion and end up with funding Zoological Parks and a major Presidential Campaign will go through this process of "Creating the Candidate and the Campaign" to win at least 50.1% of the vote on Election Night. The playbook will change as the campaign unfolds, but the process of polling, positioning, and posturing remains the same until the victory or concession speeches are made.

Is it always this way? Seldom if ever in the last thirty years has a candidate reached the race for the Presidency without some major assembly required. Jimmy Carter may have claimed to be a nuclear physicist but his playbook writers turned him into a flannel-clad peanut farmer. Ronald Reagan was a cowboy who came to the game almost ready for prime-time. Even with his core ideology so well defined, Reagan was still surrounded by some of the best playbook writers in history.

So here is a key reality from behind the scenes:

"Most political candidates are a work in progress. Their core ideology may be solid or soft, but their positions on the issues are in a constant state of flux. They may not change their position but they may highly nuance their statements and actions depending on the audience, the season, and the polling."

<u>"Well, I Just Want Someone Who Says What He Means and Means What He Says."</u>

You and about 200 million other Americans agree. On a rare occasion that actually happens, but when it does, the candidate is just as likely to get hammered by the media and the opposition for being "too self-confident, stubborn and insensitive." Pollsters and consultants don't want their candidates to be too sure of themselves out there on the stump. After all, if they really had their core identity well-defined and packaged, why would they need all the professional strategists?

Candidates fall into this "stay in the middle of the road" strategy for understandable reasons. On the right, George W. Bush gets blasted for being stubborn on Iraq. On the left Hillary Clinton gets blasted for her life-long support for abortion rights. Politicians get tired of getting slammed from the opposition and often fall into the trap of trying to ease the intensity of opposition and "make nice" to those opposing them. It's just human nature to want to come in from the rain of criticism. This is the real world of what happens inside the black limos as the candidate drives away from the rally. This is what they sit up at night thinking about. The focus always remains: "How do I reconcile my positions on the issues with the need to keep my base of 50.1% in public support?"

Of course, it doesn't help much when the electronic media is also paying polling companies to survey public opinion. Several times each year the TV news divisions and major papers pay for polls that rate the President's popularity. Just in case the President wasn't paying close enough attention, the news media shoves the polls right under the door of the Oval Office. The polls usually cover popularity ratings for Congress as well.

This is why members of Congress send out such wishy-washy form-letters when constituents write in complaining about specific issues. They are constantly thinking about staying in office. Every two years members of the House are up for re-election. Senators have a longer term of six years so they count on people forgetting controversial issues, but even with that advantage, Senators still send out wishy-washy form-letters to concerned constituents.

House and Senate staffers have to keep a very close watch on "the people back home" to make certain their bosses don't get caught in painful political cross fires. Granted, incumbents in Congress are re-elected at astoundingly high rates, even though most polls show Congress has an abysmal approval rating. Part of this re-election phenomenon is careful issue management. Many members do whatever it takes to keep that base of 50.1% - the number that keeps them in power. Avoid controversy, stay in the middle, keep 50.1% happy and we all get paid.

The candidate running for the White House is caught in the same churn. If the candidate gets elected, they start running for a second term fairly soon and the process begins all over again. In the case of the Presidency, largely due to constitutional term limits, the incumbent has a rare political opportunity to actually govern in the second term. Since no incumbent can run for a third term, the President can break free from the playbook and lead according to the dictates of conscience, ideology, conviction or whim and fancy if Congress and the media permit. The only problem is, by the time the Candidate turned President is in the second term of office, their administration is usually so fractured they can hardly govern at all. Plus, the media turns away from the second term Presidency and places most of its focus on who the next candidates will be to enter the fray for the White House.

So, is there no hope for a candidate to emerge that is genuine and will govern?

Let's try to define genuine as one held up to the light of day and found to be the genuine article. Will that candidate be found flawless under such inspection?

Chances are high that no such perfect candidate will be found. In a land dominated by movie heroes and happy endings, it is easy to understand why Americans want a President who saves the day and rides off into the sunset on either a great horse or a really sweet Harley.

Here is another key reality from behind the scenes:

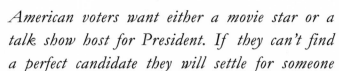

American voters want either a movie star or a talk show host for President. If they can't find a perfect candidate they will settle for someone who can come on TV and make them feel better.

Is such an expectation realistic? Of course not, but that doesn't keep America from wishing it were so. Every forty years someone comes along and re-kindles the fantasy. Franklin Delano Roosevelt held America's heart in his hand as he spoke from the fireside into the homes of America at war. Ronald Reagan could raise a tear or lift a heart as he reflected upon the shining city on a hill. That's what "we the people" want. We want inspired leadership. We look for it, we hope for it and every four years we go to the polling place staring into the harsh reality that genuine, inspiring leadership is very hard to find. (Especially in a system that permits only two individuals to emerge as candidates for the Presidency, which we will return to later.)

So if I cannot find the perfect candidate on the ballot this year what am I to do? Should I turn around and go home? Was I foolish to even imagine such a candidate could ever appear? If my choice is between the perfect candidate I hope for, or nothing, then I guess I have to settle for nothing again this year?

Chapter Three
The Lessons of History
The Perfect or Nothing – Continued

Did you know that Abraham Lincoln permitted his wife to hold séances in the White House and that Lincoln actually attended at least one of these events? [1]

The purpose of raising this little known historical fact is to once again point out the difficulty in assuming how an elected official, especially the President, will behave once in office. Given such uncertainty, perhaps it is time for media personalities, spokespeople and especially Christian leaders to step back from the battlefield and try to gain some perspective.

Christian and Jewish Scriptures both teach the doctrine of original sin. This core principle means mankind is fallen, lost, or functioning today at a level below what God originally had in mind. Thus, man is fallen, or bent and incapable of reaching perfection on his own. The Founders of America were strong advocates of this basic doctrine. They knew mankind was fallen. They had read and witnessed the cruelty of fallen human nature. They had real experience with tyranny and torture on all sides of the political equation. James Madison, often referred to as the "Father of the Constitution," summed up generations of wisdom when he stated

1. http://www.whitehouse.gov/ask/20031031-2.html

in the Federalist Papers, "If men were angels we would need no laws."

Key lesson of history:

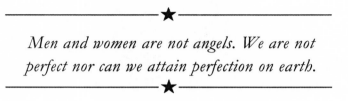

Men and women are not angels. We are not perfect nor can we attain perfection on earth.

Yet herein lies a great modern irony: Almost everyone, including Bible-believing people (who readily acknowledge the fallen nature of man) keeps looking for a perfect political candidate to run for President of the United States. Madison would not have said it quite this way, but surely Seinfeld would query: *What's up with that?*

Is it possible that Americans take the Presidency too seriously and thereby place too much pressure on themselves and the Office?

When the Republic began, the office of the Chief Executive certainly carried great significance. The new nation had to be held together in the midst of great internal and external challenges. Any new venture requires strong leadership from the top and the Founders understood this reality, but they didn't stop there. As the Constitution was constructed, they placed a huge emphasis on rightly discerning the proper role for the federal government. They wanted the balance of American power to remain with the people and their respective states. Yes, the Presidency was important, especially in the earliest years of the Republic, but the system was designed with two critical points of balance in mind.

First, the President would not be a king. He would not be called "Majesty" because he was not majestic. He would not be elected to "rule over us," but would have limited power. His office was one of three branches of government that would function in a system of checks and balances. Second, the primary political power of America would remain in the states. It was the states that came together and created this limited system of federal government, not the other way around.

Somewhere on the way to the 21st Century we lost much of this original design. Some claim it was the Civil War. Some say it was the rise of the Judiciary. Some simply blame it on digital media and 24-hour news cycles. But regardless of the causes, the question remains: Do Americans take the office of the Presidency too seriously?

Yes, it sounds heretical, especially in light of the size of the federal bureaucracy, the national debt, the war on terror, etc., etc., etc. Yes, it sounds heretical, when Americans spend months absorbing endless sound bites fed from campaign playbooks. We are saturated with bumper stickers, yard signs and lapel pins. We feed off the race that becomes bigger than a dozen Super Bowls. We have our children vote on the race in school, then we actually publish those results and call them statistically significant.

Every four years we treat the Presidential Election as if it is a referendum on the American soul. What would Washington, Madison, Jefferson and Adams say if they were sitting at the kitchen table of the average American home at election time? How would they teach a history class on the Presidency to our children? Might they not ponder how much better America could be served if we placed more emphasis on electing members of Congress instead of focusing simply on the Executive Branch? Might they not ask us, "What of your State Legislatures and your Governors?"

America was designed to function best from "the bottom-up." Washington D.C. is the last stop on the public policy train. What happens in local communities and the states is far more important on the whole than the singular race for the Presidency. Real change comes from the states. Sure, that seems hard to believe today because the media focuses endless attention on the top of the political food chain. The truth is, if Americans spent eight years fully committed to electing independent thinking people, fully dedicated to Constitutional principles, to Congress and State Legislatures, we would see a true reformation begin. Here's another clue: If people started sending more money to local organizations, state-based operations and local candidates than they do to national efforts, the change would be dramatic, immediate and long lasting. Investing in the bottom changes life at the top.

Is it possible that voters add even more pressure to the process for fear of voting for "the wrong" candidate? Do "evangelical" voters carry even bigger burdens to the polls?

The Scriptures are quite clear that convicting people of guilt is the supernatural role of the Holy Spirit of God. It is a divine process designed for redemptive purposes. In modern political circles using guilt and manipulation is hardly a tool left to the Divine. Consider this conversation which reoccurs somewhere in America every four years:

"How could you possibly vote for him? Don't you know what the Scriptures

say about (name an issue)?"

"But I am trying to pick the candidate that will do the least harm on that issue. I know it is a choice between two evils."

"Where do you find choosing evil a commandment in the Bible? How can you dare to choose any form of evil? You cannot vote for evil and possibly honor the God of the Bible?"

There are two key elements to unpacking this ravaging line of argument. The first is to return to the previous theme of the perfect or nothing. Can there be a perfect candidate on any given issue? If there are no perfect people, but all are indeed fallen, then doesn't logic tend to conclude that every candidate may have or could develop an imperfection on a given issue? Has there ever been a "perfect" candidate who, on any given issue, gave all they could 24/7 over four straight years without fail? Is there a President who used all his power to advance a particular issue in America and left office knowing there was nothing more that could have been done or done better? Is there any candidate who has not been dinked somewhere by evil?

Some people can still remember the rise of "The Silent Majority" in the 1960's. This group, which focused on law and order issues and anti-Communism, was filled with religious conservatives. They played a significant role in the landslide election of Richard Nixon. In that election Dr. Billy Graham was often seen as a supporter of Nixon, who might have been judged as the consensus candidate for Bible-believing voters. This is the same Richard Nixon who resigned in disgrace from the Presidency.

On the other end of the spectrum, evangelical voters were fascinated to discover Jimmy Carter as the first candidate to openly express his faith in terms of being "born again." In the high point of the Jesus Movement that swept the nation, many evangelicals responded to the common language being spoken by the Governor of Georgia. Four years later, many evangelical leaders were on a completely different bandwagon supporting Ronald Reagan's successful bid to unseat President Carter, who remains a lightning rod of controversy for evangelicals.

Shouldn't Christians only vote for a Christian to be President? This is the second big question. In the Founding Era, matters of personal faith were very important in the selection of leaders. The Founders would have considered "godlessness" or atheism a certain disqualifying trait for any leader. It was not a religious test. It would have been more a question of intelligence and character. Early Americans understood the connection between worldview and governance. Perhaps that is why they forwarded such outstanding leaders. But their leaders were far from perfect believers. The horrid blind spot of slavery touched many of their lives. Some early Presidents like Thomas Jefferson would be skewered by many modern evangelicals today, even though Jefferson attended church at the Capitol, read the Bible and wrote public prayers in the name of Jesus.

But doesn't the Bible teach that for Christians there is a different standard? Shouldn't Christians only vote for Christians to "rule over us?" When the New Testament was written, only a few people were able to vote for civil leaders in the Roman Empire. The Emperor was considered Divine. The "citizens" were not exactly at his level. Therefore, the writers of the New Testament did not write a verse or specific instruction on how Christians should vote in a representative Constitutional Republic. One did not exist at the time.

28

This is not to say the Bible is silent on this matter. The Old Testament provides important insight on a form of government based on law, not on emperors or kings. The Founders looked to the Old Testament model and principles in assembling the Constitution.

In a Constitutional Republic the President and the Congress do not "rule over" the people. America is a nation governed by law, not by the dictates of the ruling class. All people are supposed to be on equal ground before the law. That concept is found in the Bible throughout both the Old and New Testament. The rule of law based upon transcendent or revealed Truth is a Biblical concept that is the heartbeat of the Declaration of Independence, the Constitution and the foundation of state government.

Lots of candidates claim to be Christians. Richard Nixon was a Quaker. Jimmy Carter and Bill Clinton claimed to be born again Southern Baptists who attended Billy Graham crusades. Ronald Reagan seemed to have a problem with going to church, yet he was the clear choice of evangelical leaders. What happens if every candidate running for the White House claims to be a Christian? Do we have an obligation to press beyond labels and focus on the worldview, character and accomplishments of those seeking elected office?

The American system of government is truth-based, not man-based. The proof is in the Declaration of Independence. The Founders would not vote for atheists to represent them because the Founders were not atheists. The beauty of the system, however, is that even the professing atheist is not prohibited from running or holding office. The question is not can an atheist run for public office, but why are they running for public office?

So can a moment of honesty prevail? Regardless of party labels, TV commercials, stump speeches and promises—any imperfect, fallen person can fail to deliver on promises and prove to be a total failure in office. The only way to not vote between the lesser of two or three or four evils is to have a perfect candidate running for office.

At last check, the only perfect individual departed the earth over 2000 years ago. Jesus Christ is not returning for the purpose of running for the Presidency of the United States. So the answer must be slightly more complicated.

Chapter Four
God and Caesar

What if politics could be handled like a sock drawer? We sort the issues like socks, match them up and fold them away for later use. Wouldn't it be nice to compartmentalize political matters, to place all the political stuff of life in a little drawer and deal with it only when absolutely necessary?

Maybe the concept of the separation of church and state is supposed to work like the sock drawer. Issues that relate to the church or religion or God go in one drawer, and matters concerning the state are placed in a separate drawer. The two realms are never to intersect, match up or connect.

Maybe God won't vote this year because He doesn't really pay much attention to politics. Maybe God sees the world here below as of no real consequence. Perhaps the goal of "godliness" should be to divorce all earthly concerns and focus solely on heaven. Perhaps the wall of separation reaches all the way to heaven where God sits on His side as a casual observer of earth below. This would seem a strange place to find the God of the Bible, who sent His only Son to earth to dwell among mankind. Perhaps the life and teachings of Jesus shed light on this question of separation of a divided world.

There is a familiar passage of the New Testament that is quoted quite frequently these days. It might be the single most tortured

31

verse in political and religious debate. Religious people concerned mostly with heaven and holiness quote this verse all the time. Their counterparts on the other end of the spectrum, the secular modernists, quote the very same verse, but for different purposes. The text comes from a debate held by Jesus and a coalition marshaled against Him.

The debate occurred in the last week of Jesus' life. The setting is the Temple area in Jerusalem. Plenty of people heard the discussion, including the apostles and other followers of Jesus. The debate was a staged event planned by two political parties: the Herodians and the Pharisees. These two groups had little in common except a mutual commitment to get rid of Jesus. The Pharisees were Israelites with strong religious and national ties. They hated Roman rule over the Jewish nation. The Herodians were backers of the Herods, a family placed in power by the Romans to rule over the Jews. On any given day these two groups despised each other, but they came together in a plot to trap Jesus and expose him to potential prosecution.

Their setup began with a public question presented to Jesus. Their hope was to trap him with His own words. The question, whether it was right to pay taxes to Caesar or not, seems almost elementary to a 21st century reader. To the first century audience, this question was a toxic trap. If Jesus agreed it was right to pay taxes to Rome, then He would be viewed as anti-Israel and despised as siding with the Herodians. If He said it was wrong to pay taxes, then He could be brought up on civil charges of treason. The question combined religious doctrine, political perspectives, and civil law into a perfect no-win riddle.

Jesus proceeds into this dynamic dialogue. First, He asks His questioners for the specific coin used to pay the tax. Holding it in

His hand, He asks the questioners to tell Him what is stamped on the coin. Of course, He knew the answer. His opponents answered that it was Caesars's head and inscription. Most likely the coin included the words "Tiberius Caesar Augustus, son of the most high Augustus."

Jesus was walking deeper into the trap. The very statement on the coin was idolatry to the Jews. Caesar was not divine. You didn't need to be a Jewish legal expert to see the fallacy of Roman Emperor worship. To acknowledge the legitimacy of that coin and its message was blasphemous. To deny it was civil treason. Jesus was caught, or so it seemed, until he delivered this riddle for an answer: "Render unto Caesar the things that are Caesar's and to God the things that are God's." (KJV) See Mark 12 and Matthew 22 for the full account.

The crowd in Roman-occupied Israel that day understood the tensions contained in both the question and Jesus' answer. Unfortunately, modern believers and unbelievers alike rip this statement of Jesus out of context and interpret the riddle to suit their liking. Both camps twist this verse to support a doctrine of compartmentalization. God's stuff goes in one drawer and Caesar's into another. In this interpretation the world is divided between the sacred and the secular. Jesus was saying these two rival authorities, God and Government or the Church and the State, are competing rivals that cannot be reconciled, so they must be separated.

Some modern Christians will extend this premise to say that Jesus was dismissing the secular world and in particular the realm of civil government. He was saying forget about Caesar and the state. Give Caesar whatever he wants and move on to serving God for only God is truly important anyway. The modern secularist will usually question the existence of Jesus but for argument's sake will twist Jesus' words as well. The secularist will contend that even Jesus taught religion and politics don't mix, citing this verse as a proof text. Both groups miss the historical and Biblical context of the text and thereby largely miss the point.

Was Jesus trying to separate the world into two distinct categories? Does the Bible teach there is a sacred "God-zone" that is completely disconnected from all things earthly and political? Is that what Jesus meant to say?

Such a response would run contrary to the teachings of the Old Testament upon which Jesus' life and ministry was based. Consider just one summary text that unifies the whole of Biblical teaching on this matter: "The earth is the Lord's and everything in it, the world and all who live in it…" (Psalm 24:1a) According to this verse everything is everything and all is all, including the realm of civil government and Caesar.

The words of the risen Christ resonate with this text, when in Matthew 28:18 Jesus begins the Great Commission with this statement, "All authority in heaven and on earth has been given to me." Here again, all means all, including authority over civil government and the Church.

The whole of Scripture is quite clear that this world and the one to come all belong to God. There is no division in ownership. It's all His – but He has delegated the care of this planet to mankind, including the maintenance of both the Church and the State. Both are human institutions, made up of people, who carry the responsibility to manage both the realm of spirit and law according to God's principles.

Surely someone in the crowd that day was jumping up and down wanting to ask the next obvious question. "Jesus, what exactly is Caesar's and what is God's?" Perhaps the text fails to record this question because the first century participants knew the answer. They did not subscribe to a divided worldview. They knew the question was a trick, not based in reality at all, but designed to trip Jesus on a technicality over taxes. Had someone asked the question out loud, one could almost imagine Jesus flipping the coin to the questioner and saying: "You can figure that one out yourself."

Jesus refused to fall into the trap of compartmentalization or radical separation. The proposition of picking God or Caesar, heaven or earth, time or eternity, Church or State was rejected by Jesus. This was not just an artful dodge of a tricky question. The Bible teaches no such "either-or" worldview. Instead the totality of Scripture, including the teachings of Jesus are quite clearly unified into a "both-and" worldview. God is in His heaven and dwells here on earth with mankind. Time and eternity belong to Him. The Church and the State are both institutions He created and both have a vital role in human existence and can work together in principled balance.

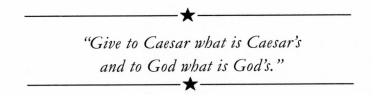

*"Give to Caesar what is Caesar's
and to God what is God's."*

"Render unto Caesar" is often quoted as a proof text to show that Jesus "was not political;" therefore His followers should not be involved in politics either. If "political" means Jesus was not a partisan member of the Pharisees, Sadducees, Herodians, Zealots,

35

or any other religious, political movement of the moment then it is true, Jesus was not "political." To claim Jesus had no interest or impact on the political process, once again grossly misses the point. If Jesus had no political impact then why did a political alliance of Jews and Romans prosecute and execute Him for claiming to be a King? A charge which Jesus did not duck or attempt to nuance.

"Are you the king of the Jews?" Pilate queried.

"Is that your own idea or did others talk to you about me? Jesus replied.

"Am I a Jew?" Pilate replied. "Your people handed you over to me. What is it you have done?"

"My kingdom is not of this world. If it were my servants would fight to prevent my arrest by the Jews, but now my kingdom is from another place," Jesus said.

"So you are a king, then!"

Jesus answered, "You are correct in saying I am a king. In fact, for this reason I was born and for this I came into the world, to testify to the truth. Everyone on the side of truth listens to me."

"What is truth?" Pilate asked. (Excerpts from John 18)

This must be the proof text that Jesus was not political. He plainly said His kingdom is "not of this world." Jesus and Pilate were not standing on equal ground. Jesus was coming from a whole different place. His Kingdom, His authority to govern was not ordered, arranged, or directed by things of this earth. He was the very revelation of transcendent Truth. A few weeks after His resurrection, Jesus would state, "All authority in heaven and earth has been given unto Me." (Matthew 28:18) Did that authority fail to include the realm of civil government? As the Son of God, would He not be a part of the ownership God holds over the whole world as depicted in Psalm 24:1? Is it not much more likely that

Jesus was telling Pilate to look up, look around, and get a clue that the trial he was prosecuting was about something much bigger than he realized? Jesus' Kingship was not based on Roman power or anchored in human politics. He was not leading a movement. He was the movement. Jesus stood before Pilate as the Truth. A message Pilate tragically missed.

"But Jesus still did not lead a revolt against Roman rule!" is the final grasp at one last straw to prove Jesus was not "political". His "servants", both human and angelic, did not fight on the day of His trail before Pilate. The former were not ready, the latter knew better. Rome did fall, however, and not simply by barbarian attacks from without. Three hundred years later, the exhausted Roman worldview of pagan gods and Caesar worship would finally succumb to the Truth which Pilate failed to see on the first Good Friday.

Pilate, the Caesars, and the government on which they stood faded away. Jesus Christ and His kingdom remain.

How does this message apply to the American equation of civil government? America's founders were not confused by an "either/or" worldview that attempts to divide the world between sacred and secular. An honest reading of their lives and writings shows they were not atheists, or even deists. They largely believed in a Creator God, who governs in the affairs of men. Not all were convinced but a Biblical worldview was the cultural consensus. The Founders sought the balance of a "both/and" perspective. They recognized civil government and the church as separate but equally important institutions. They manifestly acknowledged the existence of the Creator in the Declaration of Independence and took care to note that civil rights flow from the Creator to individuals. They made no place for government to assume the role of "rights provider." They acknowledged the authority for civil government flowed from the Creator to the individual, and from the individual to the community, by the consent of the governed. It was the people that established governments by constitutional law and legislative bodies that created specific laws on behalf of the people. Thankfully, early Americans founded many of those laws on principles revealed by the Scriptures.

There was no argument that laws against murder violated the separation of church and state because the Bible teaches "Thou shalt not kill." No one stood up and threatened a lawsuit if measures were passed to protect personal property simply because the Bible said "Thou shalt not steal." The concepts of limited government and balance of powers did not fail to make the Constitution because those laws emanate from the doctrine of original sin and the fall of man. No one sued James Madison, father of the Constitution because he dared to write, "If men were angels, we'd need no laws."

In the Founding generations the focus was not on radical separation but on balanced unity. The Founders suffered little of the political schizophrenia affecting Americans today regarding the role of the church and the state. When they wrote the First Amendment there was no attempt to build a wall that would keep religious thought from impacting public policy or ban religious expression from the public square. The term "wall of separation" was unknown when the Constitution and Bill of Rights were written. Six years later, Thomas Jefferson would use the term in a private letter to a group of Danbury Baptists who were afraid the power of the state might be used to limit the rights of the church.

Jefferson assured them the federal constitution would not permit such an abuse of power.

————————————————★————————————————

"Congress shall make no law respecting an establishment of religion, or prohibiting the free exercise thereof; or abridging the freedom of speech, or of the press; or the right of the people peaceably to assemble, and to petition the government for a redress of grievances." First Amendment to the US Constitution

————————————————★————————————————

In America, the church does not and should not attempt to usurp the rule of constitutional law and assume the duties of civil government. Civil government likewise has no constitutional authority to usurp the role of the church. Individual citizens and communities have every right and responsibility to build and shape civil government through the representative system, the Courts and by voting. Citizens, according to both the Declaration and the Constitution, also have the right to object, petition, and even deconstruct and rebuild the government if it fails to uphold their God-given rights. In America the people created the government and they did so under the watchful eye of the Creator.

To see the balance of such a "both/and" approach to God and government, one need look no farther than pocket or purse. Look at the words on American coins and dollars, the currency used to pay "Caesar" today. You will find no statement of worship for the divine Caesar, no worship of the state or the government. Instead, there is stamped a reminder, a national motto which states most simply: "In God We Trust."

So voters should not be fearful to bring their convictions to the polling place on Election Day. There is no wall of separation inside the voting booth to force people of faith to leave their principles and judgments in the drawer at home.

Chapter Five
Judge Not...

Perhaps the second most distorted Bible verse in the modern political debate comes from Matthew 7:1, where Jesus states: "Do not judge, or you too will be judged." The words roll off American tongues as easily as "Take me out to the ball game," or "I pledge allegiance to the flag" or "Where's the remote?" Unfortunately, the words have become a banner statement to justify all sorts of human behavior that Jesus Himself clearly did not condone or advocate.

Using a single line from any teacher as a universal cliché is bad form in the least. When the Teacher happens to be Jesus Christ and the text is the Sermon on the Mount, a cliché application is likely to create serious damage. Such is the case today.

First, consider the verse in context:

"Do not judge, or you too will be judged. For in the same way you judge others, you will be judged, and with the measure you use, it will be measured to you."

Admittedly it is much easier to just say the first sentence and leave the second unsaid. It certainly makes for easier printing on t-shirts and bumper stickers. The truth, however, is a bit more complicated than the common cliché. One of the dominant themes of Jesus' life and ministry was pointing to the truth of the Scriptures and exposing the hypocrisy of religious teaching and practice that fell short of the truth. Jesus reserved His harshest criticism for those who taught the words of the Bible but failed to live those words out in practice. He was not condemning mere human sinfulness or weakness. He was attacking those who hypocritically condemned sin in others while excusing sin for their own personal use and purposes. Jesus reserved His greatest anger and harshest attacks on those religious leaders who practiced such hypocrisy. He used their well-known hypocrisy as a public editorial to point people back to the pure path of Godly living. He used the power of contrast to brighten Old Testament teachings and restore their meaning.

One thing Jesus assured His followers was that He was not attempting to reconstruct the Jewish Scriptures. He was not using an eraser on the Torah. He was living out the fulfillment of the Law and the Prophets, thus He was not setting Himself up in contradiction to what had been first written in the Old Covenant. Therefore, the words of Jesus in Matthew 7 could not possibly contradict these words from Leviticus 19:15:

---★---

"Do not pervert justice, do not show partiality to the poor or favoritism to the great, but judge your neighbor fairly."

---★---

"Do not judge, or you too will be judged. For in the same way you judge others, you will be judged, and with the measure you use, it will be measured to you." Matthew 7:1

The only way to rectify these two verses is to once again see the wisdom of the "both/and" approach. Both verses make perfect sense if read in balance and in full textual and historical context. Jesus' teaching was based on Leviticus 19:15. He was not saying don't ever make a judgment or render a judicial decision regarding your neighbor. If that was the case then how would any decision of civil government be valid? Taking Jesus' words out of context and to the extreme creates a condition of personal and societal anarchy. Such an extension was obviously not the intention of Jesus or the writers of the New Testament.

Such an extension might be close to describing the destiny of secular modernist thinking. This worldview excludes the possibility of transcendent truth intersecting the human experience. The universe is closed to the potential of a Creator, First Cause, Supreme Being or anyone else being "out there" at all. In this closed system of reality the only ultimate voice is the one inside the human mind. If each man is to be his own personal deity, then how can there be a scale of value upon which to make judgments about human behavior. If one man wants no wife and another wants five, who is to judge? If one person wants to take his neighbors' property then who is to judge that action as inappropriate? "Judge not, that you be not judged," taken to the extreme would create a chaos never

43

envisioned nor intended by teachings of Jesus or the balance of the Old and New Testaments. Yet that verse is used as a battering ram in American culture every single day.

Jesus' teaching seen in context makes much more sense. He was clearly urging that judgments made about others must be made fairly without hypocrisy. In that very same passage He goes on to question why someone would try to take a speck of sawdust out of their neighbor's eye while they are carrying a plank in their own eye. This clearly illustrates the deeper meaning of Christ's teaching about hypocritical judgments.

This is obviously an important principle when it comes to voting. If Jesus were teaching to never make a judgment about another's behavior, performance or reputation then how would people ever determine who to vote for?

It is not wrong nor "judgemental" nor intolerant to question a candidate's qualifications based on his/her lifestyle. It is not hypocritical to challenge inconsistencies between what politicians say and do. The key is to judge fairly, without double standards or hidden agendas.

This is particularly important when it comes to candidate conversions on important issues, often termed "flip-flops." Do candidates have campaign conversions and change positions on issues to gain more votes? Of course they do. Sometimes they even change their positions based on the audience they are talking to, though in today's 24-hour news cycle it is a lot tougher to get away with that kind of waffling. The more substantial question is, "What about candidates who switch positions on major issues like abortion, taxes, school choice, gun-control or the definition of marriage?"

Political consultants live for flip-flops. If a campaign team can get their opponent on the waffle iron they will burn him to a crisp with TV and radio spots. Here is a real life, well-documented example from a major campaign. In 1990, George Voinovich wanted to run for Governor of Ohio. As Mayor of Cleveland he had a good track record as an honest family man with decent principles. He ran and won for Mayor as a Republican in a Democrat town. He helped turn Cleveland into a comeback city. In 1988, he took on incumbent Democrat US Senator Howard Metzenbaum in the 1988 Senate race and had his head handed to him on a platter. Very few people believed Voinovich could come back and win a statewide race for Governor two years later. Voinovich entered the race for Governor as an underdog.

He was up against a very popular Democrat, also from the stronghold of Northern Ohio, named Tony Celebreeze. As Attorney General, Celebreeze was viewed as a conservative Democrat and was the clear favorite in the race. For some reason, known only to a few insiders, Celebreeze, a Roman Catholic and lifetime pro-life candidate, decided to switch his position on abortion as the campaign began. Experts speculated it was the "time" to do so because Ohio was going progressive on abortion. Others projected the female vote would carry Celebreeze in a close race and the female vote was pro-abortion.

The Voinovich campaign team seized on the flip-flop and created a series of commercials that belong in the media hall of fame. In Ohio they came to be known as the commercials that sent the Celebreeze campaign "straight to hell." After focusing on the flip-flop with black and white shots and a grueling voice over, the spot closed with a total screen fade sucked into the vortex of a tiny white dot which then disappeared to black. The commercial raised

45

this question: "If Tony Celebreeze would sell out his deepest core values just to get a few votes today, how much more will he sell out if he ever becomes Governor?" These spots and a brilliant comeback performance in the televised debates won Voinovich the Governor's race in Ohio.

Candidates, consultants and media people don't forget moments like this. It becomes the stuff of legend and gets filed in the strategy notebooks under "flip-flopping on abortion – very dangerous." And so it should be. If a candidate is switching positions on matters of such principle to simply fit into a pollster's plans they should get hoisted up on the charge of hypocrisy. Let the negative commercials roll. But what about the candidate who sincerely comes to a change of mind and heart on a serious issue like abortion? Consider another example from a state not named to protect sources.

Several Republican candidates are vying for the nomination for statewide office. One is a former Democrat who converted to Republicanism years ago. The second candidate used to be pro-abortion but genuinely changed their position and became pro-life years ago. They went so far as to write up their "conversion" in a pro-life publication to make sure the world knew their new perspective. The conversion was based on a continual outreach of pro-lifers to this person. Their efforts succeeded. The third candidate is known as pro-abortion but pro-lifers inside the camp know this person has been seriously conflicted on the issue for years and is looking for a way to come to the pro-life position.

In the ensuing primary campaign the former Democrat, now pro-life Republican, accurately attacks the third candidate as being pro-choice. He also attacks the second candidate for being a flip-flopper on the issue and not to be trusted. The former Democrat's team decides they will be the 800 lb. guerilla on the abortion issue and blow away their challengers and win the primary, which in fact they do. The result of their tactics leaves a bitter wedge in the pro-life community. People who spend lifetimes behind the scenes building relationships with leaders and trying to convince them of the pro-life position are badly burned. The idea of reaching out and making converts is thoroughly trashed. In the worst case, the candidate that was actually trying to find a way to come out to a pro-life position, because of a true change of heart, decided doing so would never be possible. No matter how hard that candidate would try to explain the sincerity of conversion on the issue – no one would believe the story and the consultants would have a field day.

The moral of this real life story? If we are to judge our neighbor fairly (and these candidates are our neighbors, not just some product), then we must acknowledge a person's right to change their position. Who among us was born perfect on every issue? Who has arrived at the point of total political consciousness? Even more important, people who come to the light on serious issues must believe they are going to be welcomed, not hammered for showing up too late. Yes, like all candidates they must be held accountable. We are not talking about being cream puffs here. Certainly there is the risk that candidates will lie about their position and go back on their word once elected. Unfortunately, that is the risk integrity requires. That's what we have elections for. When an elected official lies and goes back on their word that's when you find another candidate, call in the consultants and let the negative ads roll.

If we are to judge our neighbor fairly, we must be willing to give people the hope of changing and being warmly rewarded for coming to the wiser choice on key issues. This goes for candidates of all parties. There are people registered as Democrats who may actually agree with conservative Republicans on serious issues. There are Republicans who are far to the left of many Democrats. Shouldn't we judge a candidate based on his/her issue positions and performance not their party label? Would the pro-life or pro-marriage community be sad if every candidate running for the White House was both pro-life and pro-marriage?

Both the Old and New Testament provide additional insight on qualifications for "judging" or rightly discerning those who should hold leadership positions. Moses faced this question and answered it with the help of his father-in-law Jethro. The burden of settling disputes among the Israelites was wearing Moses out, so his father-in law made a few suggestions. He instructed Moses to teach the people how to obey God's commandments and to select men to establish an effective judicial system for the nation of Israel. Moses took the advice and appointed judges from among all the people who were: 1) capable 2) feared God 3) trustworthy and 4) hated dishonest gain. In this formulation of the Israelite judicial system we see a form of representative government emerging from the book of Exodus and we see a grid of qualifications for judging qualified leaders. (See Exodus 18 for more details.)

In the New Testament, the Presbytery or elder council was a leadership body that governed congregational life. The deacons also shared a representative role of leadership for New Testament communities. While these bodies were not and should not be confused with leadership roles in civil government, there are lists of characteristics provided that the Apostles and St. Paul considered strong requirements for good leadership. Those lists can be found in the book of Acts and First Timothy. The lists are not cited here to avoid confusion. The threshold for leadership is very high in the governing structures of the New Testament church. Just reading the list causes one to shudder at the responsibility placed upon those who follow the calling to leadership in the Church. Very few of even America's greatest political leaders have ever matched up to the qualifications for Church leadership. America would be greatly served by leaders who aspired to such noble standards, but to ask this of political leaders when church leaders are struggling mightily to meet these standards could easily fall into precisely the kind of hypocrisy Jesus condemned in His teaching in the Sermon on the Mount.

As people of faith face the crisis of leadership in America, perhaps the first prayer should be one of repentance. Scandals among religious and church leaders have done serious damage to the faithful and the culture at large. Surely there are far more Christian leaders honestly, faithfully and sacrificially serving than those who have fallen, but the New Testament does not encourage a scoring system based on averages.

The second prayer should be for wisdom as voters look to elect the best leaders in the arena of civil government. It is difficult to vote for people with clearly publicized moral failures. Some will choose not to vote for any with such prior histories, which is within their voting rights. If Americans settle for only the perfect or nothing, we will surely be lonely on Election Day.

This leads to the third prayer which combines confession, repentance and commitment. The reason the choices before us on Election Day are so often unacceptable is because we the people have failed to train up, support, educate, finance, equip and encourage leaders for this nation. How could we let this happen to this city on a hill? How could we presume that leaders just grow on trees or pop up from the cabbage patch or come by delivery of the stork? Truth be told, we spend more time and money raising up athletic superstars, rock stars and movie stars than we do American leaders. Most Americans will spend far more on movie and sporting event tickets than they will ever invest in a young upcoming political leader.

So what are we to do? End the denial, repent of our foolishness and start praying for, recruiting and supporting young people who will embrace the founding ideals of America. This is the infrastructure of hope that must be rebuilt in America.

Chapter Six
The Key to the Puzzle:
The Consent of the Governed

Some puzzles have patterns. Learn the key to the pattern and the pieces begin to fit together. Since the beginning of America in July of 1776, a constant pattern flows through the American system of law and government. The Committee of five that aptly used Jefferson's pen to write the Declaration of Independence said it this way:

---★---

"We hold these truths to be self-evident, that all men are created equal, that they are endowed by their Creator with certain unalienable rights; that among these are life, liberty and the pursuit of happiness. That to secure these rights governments are instituted among men deriving their just powers from the consent of the governed."

---★---

The operative term here, the key to the pattern is: "...the consent of the governed." This is the place where civil authority is transferred from the people to elected officials under the rule of law. American Constitutional law and the British system of law dating back to the Magna Carta recognize the true source of political power flows from God the Creator, to the people who choose to delegate a portion of that power to representative forms of civil government.

Did the Founders discover this in the same jar Ben Franklin used to discover electricity? Were they just flying a theoretical kite hoping lightning would strike and a nation would form as the result?

During the one and only Constitutional Convention America has ever held, a room full of legendary minds met to create the laws that would define, establish, and limit the role of the Government of the United States. These men were sent by the colonies to represent their unique states. Again, it was "the states" that created the federal system. The credentials and amount of research done by the members of the Convention were astounding. They had many plans and had searched through government formulas throughout the ages. When deadlocked beyond resolution, Benjamin Franklin rose to address the Chair, held by General Washington. Franklin addressed the Convention with these words:

Mr. President:

The small progress we have made after four or five weeks close attendance & continual reasonings with each other — our different sentiments on almost every question, several of the last producing as many noes as ayes, is me thinks a melancholy proof of the imperfection of the Human Understanding. We indeed seem to feel our own want of political wisdom, since we have been running about in search of it. We have gone back to ancient history for models of government, and examined the different forms of those Republics which having been formed with the seeds of their own dissolution now no longer exist. And we have viewed Modern States all round Europe, but find none of their Constitutions suitable to our circumstances.

In this situation of this Assembly groping as it were in the dark to find political truth, and scarce able to distinguish it when to us, how has it happened, Sir, that we have not hitherto once thought of humbly applying to the Father of lights to illuminate our understandings? In the beginning of the contest with G. Britain, when we were sensible of danger we had daily prayer in this room for the Divine Protection. — Our prayers, Sir, were heard, and they were graciously answered. All of us who were engaged in the struggle must have observed frequent instances of a Superintending providence in our favor. To that kind providence we owe this happy opportunity of consulting in peace on the means of establishing our future national felicity. And have we now forgotten that powerful friend or do we imagine that we no longer need His assistance?

I have lived, Sir, a long time and the longer I live, the more convincing proofs I see of this truth — that God governs in the affairs of men. And if a sparrow cannot fall to the ground without his notice, is it probable that an empire can rise without his aid? We have been assured, Sir, in the sacred writings that "except the Lord build they labor in vain that build it." I firmly believe this; and I also believe that without his concurring aid we shall succeed in this political building no better than the Builders of Babel: We shall be divided by our little partial local interests; our projects will be confounded, and we ourselves shall be become a reproach and a bye word down to future age. And what is worse, mankind may hereafter this unfortunate instance, despair of establishing Governments by Human Wisdom, and leave it to chance, war, and conquest.

I therefore beg leave to move — that henceforth prayers imploring the assistance of Heaven, and its blessings on our deliberations, be held in this Assembly every morning before we proceed to business, and that one or more of the Clergy of this City be requested to officiate in that service.

Franklin's words remind us the Founders leaned heavily upon the Judeo-Christian tradition of law and civil order. They were unafraid to pray in public for guidance and to turn to Scripture for counsel and concepts.

One such concept, familiar to colonial pulpits, especially in the Revolutionary period, is found in I Samuel chapter 8. Here the nation of Israel had decided to challenge the wisdom of Samuel the prophet and seek a new form of government. Samuel was greatly disturbed by the consensus of the people to change forms of government and seek a political monarchy to lead the nation. He went to God with his complaint and to his surprise the Lord advised Samuel to give the people what they asked for. Give them a King to lead them just like all the other nations.

The primary moral of the story is this: Way back in the book of Genesis, God delegated the authority over the governance of the earth to mankind. From Genesis to First Samuel humankind had made a myriad of decisions on what to do with the authority of governance. God laid out a plan for ancient Israel to follow. It was contained in a covenant or testament between God and His people. It required the consent of two parties to be placed in effect. Israel had agreed with God's revealed governmental structures from the time of Moses until Samuel. They struggled mightily to uphold their end of the deal but there was no attempt to amend the plan until the eighth chapter of I Samuel.

When the people decided they wanted a change, what was the response of the Almighty? Did he throw down lightning bolts from the heavenlies? Did he strike the people with a plague? No, the Lord God gave the people what they asked for. He sent them a solemn warning of the consequences their change in governance would produce. He warned them of the inevitable abuses of fallen man holding too much power without legal accountability. The people politely listened, but they chose to amend the system and accept a King to "rule over them" like the other nations.

When the monarchy of Israel failed who was to blame? Was it the human kings who conformed to their fallen natures? Or was the real cause the corporate decision of the people who abdicated their responsibilities and delegated them to a poor form of civil government?

Biblical governance has always hinged on the rule of law and the consent of the governed. God delegated civil governance to mankind once and for all in Genesis and He has not taken it back, as of yet. People have the right to choose how they will be governed, not just in America but in the entire world. In some nations the choice is relatively easy. In others the struggle for government based upon the consent of the people is impossible short of a revolution.

America's founders witnessed the struggle for government by consent for generations. They learned the stories of the fall of Rome and the endless conflicts of the Middle Ages. They were great-great grandchildren of the Protestant Reformation and the work of the great reformers, Luther and Calvin. They got all this stuff and put it to good use. So, when they wrote the Declaration of Independence and the Constitution, the words "consent of the governed" and "We the people" were not just popular jargon or code. They were words that stood for hundreds of years of principled struggle. This is the principle upon which the entire American system rests: the consent of the governed.

So what does all this have to do with electing people to office? Let's return to the conversation that often occurs around election time:

Bill: "How can you vote for him? He is simply the lesser of two evils. I cannot and will not vote for evil, therefore I will not vote for either candidate."

Jack: "But if you do that — the more evil candidate will win and that will (pick one) a) cost more lives b) raise taxes c) destroy religious liberty d) all of the above. I am voting for the candidate that is most likely to do the least harm in the culture."

Bill: "It doesn't matter. God will not permit me to vote for evil. In fact, God is so displeased with what we have done to America that He is going to permit an evil person to become President to bring judgment upon America. Remember how He did this to ancient Israel, how he raised up hostile enemies to chasten Israel? God is going to raise-up a terrible President to judge America. The longer you prop up lesser-evil candidates with your vote, the more you delay the inevitable. Let the most evil candidate win. Let America fall. I refuse to vote for any candidate that does not meet the Biblical standards for righteousness. I fear God more than man. If America falls then real repentance will come and God will send us righteous leaders."

This is not a fantasy conversation. It rolls out every four years in American religious and political circles. Unpacking it requires untangling a mess of crossed theological wires.

First of all, the Founders largely agreed the Old and New Testaments were inspired and valid sources of Divine revelation and profitable for the governing of mankind. Spend a little time reading the textbooks used in schools back then and you'll get the picture.

The Founders did not, however, consider America to be in exactly the same relationship with God as Old Testament Israel. They turned to Old Testament teaching and principles often. They based much of American law on the Laws of Moses. They sought God's favor by obedience and feared the consequences of disobedience but they didn't ask God to appoint George Washington as the first President of the United States. They did not hold a prayer meeting and anoint John Adams as second President, nor Jefferson the third, nor Madison the fourth. They voted for President and accepted the consequences of their vote. They understood the Biblical principles of the rule of law and the consent of the governed. They were not electing a king with divine authority.

From the earliest years of the Republic, voting rights have been expanding in America so that today every citizen over the age of eighteen who is registered and not a convicted felon has the right to vote. There has never been an American election where the people waited for God Almighty to cast his ballot and that was the end of the matter.

God does not vote in America. We the People do vote and that is exactly the point. In America, the Biblical concept of the consent of the governed works out in the form of free elections.

The Founders fought a Revolutionary War to gain this right. Many battles have followed to keep expanding this right. It all goes back to the Declaration of Independence:

——————————————————————————————

"We hold these truths to be self-evident, that all men are created equal, that they are endowed by their Creator with certain unalienable rights; that among these are life, liberty and the pursuit of happiness. That to secure these rights governments are instituted among men deriving their just powers from the consent of the governed."

———————————————★———————————————

In America we each have the right to participate in the process of shaping the government. That right is a gift the Founders believed came from God the Creator. We have exactly the kind of elected officials we put into office by our actions. The Bible teaches that God governs in the affairs of men. God can veto the results of an election anytime He wishes but there is little evidence in American history that God has ever chosen to do so. Granted, a few vetoes from the Almighty along the way might have saved the nation a great deal of grief. The people of America have the God-ordained right to government based upon the consent of the governed. And like ancient Israel, we the people are responsible for the consequences of our collective decisions.

Therefore, we cannot blame God if the candidates running are not to our liking. We cannot blame God if the lesser or the greater of two evils is elected. God is not voting this year, next year or in the years to come. He gave us the right to do that for ourselves. In the long term and the short term we get exactly the kind of government we choose.

So how do we deal with that kind of responsibility? If we are not going to delegate such a burden to a King, how about just handing it off to a political party?

Chapter Seven
Political Parties
Do We Have to Go There?

The dentist, the doctor's physical, the tax audit, buying a car, renewing your driver's license – most people would rather do any of the above instead of going to a meeting of a political party. Can anyone blame them?

America was not founded on political parties. The first three elections for the Presidency were conducted without the presence of political parties. General George Washington was elected to the Presidency for two consecutive terms by a unanimous electoral vote, without the existence or endorsement of a political party. Perhaps history provides a clue as to just how united the American states were back then.

In his Farewell Address, President Washington issued several warnings to the new nation. He saved some of his strongest language for political parties, often termed "the spirit of party." He likened partisanship or affiliation to party above principle as "a dangerous fire." He was rightly concerned that once the fledgling nation was established, political leaders would become more interested in accumulating personal power than preserving the founding principles of the Declaration and the Constitution. President Washington said it this way:

"There is an opinion that parties in free countries are useful checks upon the administration of the government and serve to keep alive the spirit of liberty. This within certain limits is probably true; and in governments of a monarchical cast, patriotism may look with indulgence, if not with favor, upon the spirit of party. But in those of the popular character, in governments purely elective, it is a spirit not to be encouraged. From their natural tendency, it is certain there will always be enough of that spirit for every salutary purpose. And there being constant danger of excess, the effort ought to be by force of public opinion, to mitigate and assuage it. A fire not to be quenched, it demands a uniform vigilance to prevent its bursting into a flame, lest, instead of warming, it should consume."

By the time political parties emerged (In the era of the Jefferson Presidency) they were largely driven by ideology. Throughout history the Federalists versus the Anti-federalists, the Free Soil Party, the Whigs, and the No Nothings all had political axes to grind.

Today's political parties are different. They do not exist so much to define platforms and draw philosophical differences with opponents. Today's political parties exist not to drive ideological agendas, but for the pure concentration of power. Just listen to Democrat and Republican leaders. They equally despise the "ideologues" in both their parties. People with strong opinions on issues are seen as divisive. The Democrats' creed is inclusion and the Republicans bandy about the big tent. In both cases they want to add numbers never subtract votes. Party leaders today advocate a form of political relativism that teaches we are all OK as long as we don't seriously disagree on anything. Holding strong opinions is rarely tolerated.

Party Platforms are the play gyms where state and national leaders send the "ideologues" for exercise. Every four years both parties pretend to have a debate over issues at their national conventions. They surrender their printing presses to a futile practice called the "Party Platform." The most adamant ideologues at the convention work to control the content of the final draft. Before the ink is dry the nominees of both Parties are usually walking away from the platform as if it did not exist. State political parties are not the reservoir of ideology. Today's Party mechanisms exist to gain political offices and control political power for as long as possible. Whichever Party controls the seats of government gains the prize of controlling the federal budget and all fifty state budgets.

The size of state and federal budgets in America today is astronomical. The numbers are in the trillions of dollars. There is no company in the world that comes close to the annual budget of the US Government which is controlled by the US Congress. Few companies in the world can rival the budgets of major US states.

The people holding elected offices at the Statehouse and on Capitol Hill have phenomenal power over massive wealth – none of which is their own. They get to manage the biggest pot of somebody else's money in the history of the world. Every decision they make impacts some bureau, agency, corporation, or special interest group. Therefore, lobbyists line the halls of the Legislature waiting to remind incumbent office holders just how important they really are. Those same lobbyists work to funnel billions of dollars into the two American political parties to make certain their friends in the Legislature retain office. One hand washes the other and in the end everyone gets paid well.

To keep this wonderful game of inside baseball moving, along with everyone winning something, the incumbents of both parties have worked to structure state and federal campaign laws so that "independent" parties and candidates can only compete at a profound disadvantage. Independent voters are discriminated against in many states and denied the right to vote in many primary elections. At the same time all taxpayers are forced to pay for "party" primaries conducted by officials of the state for the exclusive benefit of Democrats and Republicans. The system is rigged, plain and simple, to keep only two parties in power and in control of trillions of tax dollars. The people writing the rules for participation are the same people holding the power today. The two major political parties share a carefully brokered monopoly over the board game of American politics. The goal of their game is not ideology. Their goal is to maintain the status quo so every player gets paid.

Don't the parties serve any valid purpose? In fact they do a few things well. They work to field candidates and raise money. They facilitate the necessary paperwork to maintain their status as major parties at the state and federal level. They fund an executive team to conduct lots of polls, raise lots of money, and keep lots of lawyers on hand to challenge the paperwork filings of their opponents. (Was the idea of raising lots of money mentioned?) Oh, one more thing, they run a made-for-television event every four years called a convention where lots of their friends get together for a week-long party. They send the taxpayers a portion of the bill for that event as well.

So why not reject political involvement and become a sideline cynic?

Because the truths described in the Declaration of Independence remain self-evident. The basic rights of each individual do not flow from government, political parties or the popular vote. The right to life, liberty, property and the pursuit of happiness flow from the Creator. Government exists to secure these rights, not provide them. Ultimately the power to build a system of governance, or rebuild it remains squarely where it began: with the consent of the governed.

Therefore, the people of America can never walk away from the process of civil government and cynically sit out the process. If "the government" we see today is wrong, if it is corrupt and out of control, if it has been hijacked by professional politicians and party users, then it is time for change. America is in this mess because generations of voters let it get this bad. If we the people do nothing it will only get worse.

The key question is not, "Why should I bother voting and be involved?" The key question is, "How do I participate in the process and make a principled difference?" The first step is not to run out and try to reform the Democrats or the Republicans, nor is it to start a new political party. The answer may not be found in a political party at all.

Chapter Eight
Where the Left and Right Both Went Wrong

Did you know Abraham Lincoln ran as a third party candidate in a four candidate race for the White House? True story, which makes it laughable when current Party leaders chastise frustrated voters who want to run independent candidates for the Presidency. Lincoln was just such a candidate and he was the first Republican candidate to run for and win the Presidency.

President Washington warned us not to get hooked on parties, but like most rebellious teenagers, we the people didn't listen. Americans have been drunk on the spirit of Party for quite a few generations. Can we at least admit the pain and suffering brutal partisanship has caused America? Can we acknowledge the number of broken bodies on the side of the road caused by the demolition derby of party politics? Can we admit that most political party leaders today are seeking power and wealth instead of principle and the common good? Can we look in the mirror and admit how many problems we have today because politicians spend their time and our money fighting over who gets the credit for any good idea?

Now that the reality therapy has begun, can we also admit another tragic mistake? Partisanship is not a disease that impacts only politicians. Far too many business, community and religious leaders from the days of the civil rights movement in the 60's to the "religious right" of the 80's have fallen into the pit of partisanship. They tried to take short cuts to power by marrying powerful social agendas into a single political party and ended up at the bottom of the pile.

Here is the lesson:

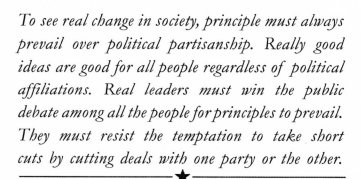

To see real change in society, principle must always prevail over political partisanship. Really good ideas are good for all people regardless of political affiliations. Real leaders must win the public debate among all the people for principles to prevail. They must resist the temptation to take short cuts by cutting deals with one party or the other.

It is easy to understand how this temptation arises. Community leaders who are on the outside of social and political credibility work very hard to build a base of public support for their issue. The issue could be abolition, women's suffrage, temperance, civil rights or any major issue that has risen up from the people and created changes in the legal system.

Issues leaders know they must build a big enough movement to get noticed. They need "the politicians" to listen to their cause. They want to be taken seriously. It is hard, lonely work. When the media finally starts to pay attention and a few victories are won, the invitation comes from "the politicians" to come inside from the cold. "Come to the Inauguration, come to the White House, come talk to us in Congress." Those invitations don't usually come from both parties. They come from the group that wants to capture the "new movement" and their voters into either the Democrat or Republican base. A modern example of this process can be found in the experience of the movement dubbed by the media as "the Religious Right."

Religious conservatives were around in the 1960's. They were called "silent" back then, but they voted. By the 1980's they were finding each other and finding the electronic media. They nearly galvanized in time to become the voting bloc that gave Jimmy Carter the Presidency in 1976. They certainly found their voice by 1980. Ronald Reagan's people saw this opportunity and moved in to capture this "new" movement on the political landscape. On Election Night 1980, the silent majority was silent no longer. Incumbent President Jimmy Carter (the born-again Southern Baptist) conceded defeat before the polls were even closed in California.

On January 20th, 1981, Washington D.C. was filled with wide-eyed evangelicals who were seeing the White House for the very first time. For the next eight years, whenever Ronald Reagan's consultants called those evangelical leaders answered. Whenever the media was looking for a debate or spokesperson the evangelical elite were ready to appear. By 1992 the "Religious Right" and their handful of high media profile leaders were viewed as a fundamental plank in the Republican infrastructure.

The truth about the "Religious Right" may not yet have been told. In fact, the handful of high profile personalities that dominated the movement in the 1980's and 90's were never as organized, coordinated or well-funded as commentators like to portray. Nor did they represent the millions of voters they claimed. The leaders of the Religious Right were expert in manipulating media. They had powerful operations in television, radio and direct mail and used them to market to a political sub-culture. They were very good at making that sub-culture look larger than life.

For the "mainstream" media it was love at first sight. The mainstream media and the religious right needed each other and fed off of each other. The Right would hold a pro-life march and the media would cover the event and underreport the number of pro-life marchers. The Right would instantly attack the Media as leftist, biased and a source of destruction and the Media would air the story all over the national and cable news. The Religious Right made a lot of news stories in the 80's and 90's.

Then came the advent of talk radio and the Right versus Left arguments continued all day and all night over the airwaves. The leaders of the Right received the attention they needed and the Media got the kind of controversy that pushes ratings and sells advertising. It was a marriage built in media heaven.

But a funny thing happened on the way to the November 1992 Election. At the height of the Religious Right's media exposure and perceived power, the Republican incumbent President George H.W. Bush lost to Democrat Bill Clinton. Then in 1996 Bill Clinton easily defeated Republican nominee Senator Bob Dole.

The Religious Right blamed the defeats on the independent candidacy of Ross Perot. In fact, Perot gained substantial votes in key battleground states. Why were Religious Right leaders unable to hold their troops together against the rising Independent tide?

Could it have been that by 1992 the elite evangelicals had read so much of their own press that they missed the growing discontent with the Republican Party? Did a large part of "the movement" they claimed as their own actually defect to Ross Perot or even worse to Democrat, Southern Baptist, Bill Clinton?

This is not to say that these leaders accomplished nothing from 1980 forward. They were motivated by an honest desire to see positive social change in America. They paid a significant price to get involved in the process and bring important issues to the table. But they did not get the changes they had hoped for. The primary reason for these failures is they committed themselves fully to work within the Republican Party alone. In several states their leaders even led charges to take over state Republican parties. They thought they could shortcut winning the consent of the governed by building a big enough single party dominance. They failed to see they were dragging their legitimate issues into the pit of partisanship.

They were being used by Republican leaders. It's one thing to be used when you know you are being used and are willing to serve. It's quite a different matter to just get used. Of course they should have known better. Maybe the bright lights, media celebrity status and fund raising budgets blinded their vision. To be sure, Republican Party leaders were not fooled. On many occasions Republican leaders were laughing out loud at the evangelicals. Republican leaders would hold endless meetings with them, listen to all their concerns and then thank them for their insights. Another meeting would be scheduled and another until evangelicals were talked out. Each time the evangelicals would report back to their constituents on how much progress was being made behind the scenes.

But the real story was this – when the evangelicals left the room, the Republican bosses just laughed out loud at the pitiful saints and did little about their issues. When challenged, the Republicans always had the same answer: "Where are the evangelicals going to go? They won't vote for Democrats. Don't worry, they will be back."

By 2000, the Religious Right claimed to have fully recovered from the era of Bill Clinton. Fueled once again by the electronic media, the evangelical elites moved to reclaim the White House. Their leaders packaged George W. Bush for the evangelical sub-culture. By a margin of 537 votes in Florida, George W. Bush defeated Al Gore. The invites to the inauguration were sent out once more and once again the "Religious Right" danced in Republican-only circles.

Karl Rove, the political guru of the Bush White House, wasn't happy though. He discerned that a large number of evangelicals stayed home in 2000. By 2004, evangelical leaders were convinced that the razor thin margin of the first Bush victory was their fault, so they set out to register voters and work on turn out. Rove had a better idea. He wanted evangelicals to have an issue so strong to take to the polls that their numbers would have to show up on Election Day. Scouring the political landscape, he found the perfect issue to exploit: the defense of marriage.

What happened in the marriage debate of 2004 is highly instructive. It points out the fundamental flaws in taking a purely partisan approach to a really good idea. First, let's talk about what could have happened. After the earthquake of homosexual unions being declared "marriage" in Massachusetts, almost any state could have passed a defense of marriage amendment. A whole lot of states did just that. When Rosie O'Donnell went to California to get married and wave her flowers in the face of the nation, the momentum for a federal marriage amendment took another leap forward.

Defending marriage began as a non-partisan idea. Back in 1996, the Congress passed a federal Defense of Marriage statute designed to protect state marriage laws. President Bill Clinton signed the measure. Plenty of Democrats voted for it. (Today Hillary Clinton is calling for the repeal of the law.)

Democrats, Republicans, and Independents all get married and many raise children in traditional families. The idea of upholding a law supported by 4,000 years of history was a pretty easy opportunity to win the consent of almost all the governed. But Karl Rove and a few Republican social issues leaders had a better idea. Why not call for a vote in Congress on a federal constitutional amendment in October of 2004. Why not turn marriage, which was a bridge building issue, into a wedge issue?

Here is the strategy they imposed. First, they called for and got a vote on a Federal Marriage Amendment in October 2004. They knew they had absolutely no chance of passing the Amendment. To do so would require super-majority votes of two-thirds of the House and Senate. That meant every Republican and a good number of Democrats would have to vote yes on the Amendment. Karl Rove knew the groundwork for that kind of bipartisan support in Congress did not exist. By calling for the vote, the White House chose to use marriage as a wedge to expose Democrats as "anti-marriage" and isolate them from the voters back home.

Next, they launched a campaign to place marriage amendments on state ballots in battleground states. They were not the least bit bashful about announcing this strategy to their base and the watching world. The idea was to get voters in key states to the polls in support of the state marriage amendments and the presumption was they would vote for George W. Bush.

Put yourself in the Democrats' shoes for just a moment. Marriage is no longer an issue of the people, a matter of faith and principle. Now it is a strategic wedge to defeat Democrat candidates. Democrats on Capitol Hill exposed the strategy and refused to vote for the amendment. Back home, they simply shamed the Republicans for such tactics and got re-elected.

Yes, George W. Bush was re-elected and some evangelical leaders claim it was the marriage amendment in Ohio that gave him the victory. President Bush carried Florida by a much larger margin than Ohio, even though Florida did not have a marriage amendment on the ballot. Ironically, the proposed amendment in Ohio, which did pass, was so hastily written and confusing that the President could never mention the measure in his Ohio campaign. George Bush won Ohio and the White House, and any hope for passing a federal marriage amendment on Capitol Hill died.

Pro-marriage leaders made a horrid mistake for their issue. They failed to realize they did not have the strength to elect members of Congress on the marriage issue. The consent of the governed was clearly in favor of marriage, but the case had not been adequately made that a federal amendment was truly necessary. When Democrats returned to Congress after the 2004 election, they determined to never give the President the votes he needed to pass the Amendment. It was proper political partisan revenge. Bush claimed he beat Democrats with marriage. Democrats would beat Bush by never giving him the ability to deliver the Amendment to his base.

On the Saturday before the second Bush Inauguration, the President pulled the plug on the Marriage Amendment. He gave an interview stating he was going to wait on Senate approval before calling for a vote on the Amendment. "Pro-family" leaders on their way to the Inaugural Ball had no idea their number one issue had just been tanked. A meaningless vote was called for in 2006. When the Democrats took majority control of Congress, the marriage issue faded into the abyss, the victim of a hyper-partisan strategy that failed.

The moral of the story – putting all your eggs into one political basket is a very dangerous strategy. It is very difficult to win the public debate, to gain the consent of the governed while proceeding as a blatant partisan. To put all your hope in one party to provide all the political candidates you will ever need is risky. To take a critical issue into the arena with a wholly partisan game plan, especially if you need a two-thirds majority of a divided Congress for passage, is just plain dumb. Turning a bridge-building issue into a partisan wedge is a good way to blow up a bridge and get left holding nothing but a meaningless wedge in your hands.

This is not to say that "wedge issues" are never a logical political strategy. The idea of using a political wedge to secure a victory by a narrow margin is not new nor inherently evil. It is incredibly risky. The truth is, any legislative or electoral victory won by slim margins will have to be won over and over again in the Legislature, the Courts, and the media. In the long run, the better path is bridge building. The consent of the governed still works. If you are going to go to all the trouble to fight to change America, why not do it the right way?

Here is the key lesson:

Winning the public debate on key issues so the majority of people support your issue is the genuine path to victory. If the consent of the governed is won on any issue, the politicians, their parties, the media, and the entire political process will follow.

Is that the fastest or easiest way to victory? That's the question several "pro-family" leaders asked years ago. They didn't like the answer, because winning the consent of the governed is the long, hard path. They chose the faster path and ended up bankrupting one of the most important issues of their generation.

Chapter Nine
A Better Plan

The American electoral system faces two very serious problems. One is long term, the other is short term. There are solutions to both. Here are 10 suggestions to address the long term problems.

Suggestion One:
Principle above party – always.

Perhaps the way to solving the long term problem of the political monopoly held by the Democrats and Republicans is to return to the lessons of the Founding Era. George Washington warned us that partisan divisions could pose a serious threat to America. Remember, these fault lines are not largely ideological. They are mostly about power and money. So a guiding light to lead America out of this wilderness would be for citizens to rediscover the Founding principles upon which America was built and stand upon those principles.

What does that look like? It means ordering or downloading a copy of the Declaration of Independence and the US Constitution and reading them. Try holding those two documents up against any political agenda brought forward by every candidate or party.

75

Judge candidates and parties by their commitment to these core documents and principles. If they don't measure up then try to patiently help them understand the American way of doing politics. If they won't listen, politely walk away. That means taking your money and your vote with you.

Don't ever let political consultants, candidates or parties make you a part of their "playbook" without your explicit consent. Don't let them ever paint you into a corner where you have "nowhere to go." You can always go to the Declaration, the Constitution, and to the voting booth and skip their race, issue, or candidate. They cannot take away your right to vote (at least not yet).

Suggestion Two:
Read some good books and learn how the system works

Good people get wiped out in this process for lack of basic knowledge. For example, if a candidate for President makes a local speech promising to deliver on a big national issue, stop and ask the question: Can the President actually do that without the vote of Congress? (The answer is: no he can't.)

Then ask yourself, how many votes can the President count on in Congress to get that major reform passed? A few minutes online will help you get a read for where Congress stands on the issue. Then, if you get the chance, you can ask the candidate how he/she plans to get Congress to pass legislation on the big promise. Then watch the fun begin. You see, they don't expect you to know how the system works.

Here is another example. Let's go back to the Federal Marriage Amendment for a moment. Proponents who called twice for doomed votes in the US Senate promised that putting senators "on the record on marriage" would impact elections back home. The presumption was that a single issue would alter enough races to create a pro-marriage majority in the US Senate.

If you read a few history books on American politics, you discover very few issues ever reach such a "national synergy" and dominate state races for the US Senate. A major war might have such impact. An economic collapse might get it done. But as former House Speaker Tip O'Neill was fond of quoting: "All politics is local." People vote for and against US Senate candidates for a whole host of reasons. In addition, every US Senator has a six-year term and those 100 members rotate their election cycles. That means if you want to fight an issue battle that will rock the Senate, you have to keep the fight going for six years to reach one full election cycle. In the US House, the dynamic is completely different. Every House member runs for re-election every two years on the same day. The US House is much more sensitive to major issue debates and the impact on voters back home.

The first part of accountability is knowledge and in politics knowledge is power. Knowing how the system works can be a huge help. Knowing a bit about history is also a great way to increase your personal power in the process. A list of enjoyable books can be found in the suggested bibliography in the appendix of this book.

Suggestion Three:
Great ideas should be invited to every Party

A good idea is good for all of America. Example: Freedom

from dependency on foreign oil is a great idea that would benefit every American. Obviously, the path to getting there has to be carefully brokered so that the Government does not create winners and losers in the transition. Both parties should be fully embracing energy independence and racing each other to create better ideas and opportunities.

To get to this highly desired spot, the leaders in the energy independence movement must resist the temptation to move to Washington D.C. and pick one party or the other for a strategic ally. They must speak to all Americans: Democrat, Republican, third party, fourth party, and Independents. There has to be an end to "special interest politics." This is a bad habit in America. Groups develop their own sub-culture and then work to lobby the government to get their agenda through the back door of the Legislature by buying up enough votes for victory. Special Interest Politics (SIP) is the antithesis of the consent of the governed.

Sometimes the votes are not bought for money. Some organizations love to build numbers and try to bully politicians into listening to them. "Our organization has ten million members, Congressman, and we all will be voting in November. So you better do what we ask you on this legislation."

What if the legislation supported by 10 million members goes against the Declaration of Independence or the Constitution? What if it is a really dumb idea? Just having numbers doesn't make a movement right. It never has. That's why the Founders never used the term "democracy" to describe America. They never wanted political leaders to do something just because the numbers were right. There has to be more. Great ideas are tied to timeless principles, and work for the common good.

Suggestion Four:
Time for more viable candidates

The two-party system in America has failed to deliver the quantity and quality of candidates needed to serve the states and nation well. This statement of course will ignite negative reactions from Party leaders across the nation. The truth is they know the statement is a correct and fair analysis.

Some of the problem is not intentional. Serving in state legislatures and in the US House of Representatives is not as easy as it looks. Members of Congress make good money and have large staff and office budgets, but the travel is brutal. Most state lawmakers get part-time pay for a job that can be very demanding. So party leaders have some excuse for the lack of candidates. They would like to find more as well.

One way to fix this problem is to shorten the length of legislative sessions at the state and federal level. Both Florida and Texas have limited legislative sessions. Other states could surely follow this example – except for the fact the politicians are afraid to admit they meet more than is truly necessary. Anything that minimizes their importance is scary to them.

The real culprit here is "we the people." In most states, independents can run and win in state legislative races. The problem is they have no network of support to help gather signatures, raise funds and turn out votes. It is especially tough when they have to compete against the monopoly candidates in the two parties.

What America needs is a revival of citizen participation akin to the work of Sam Adams, John Hancock and the original Sons (and Daughters) of Liberty. These community leaders mentored and supported community activism. They helped raise up candidates for public service. They raised money, trained people, published articles and tracts and built extraordinary networks of independent support.

Perhaps instead of fighting with the Republicans and Democrats, citizen leaders should establish their own training schools and political action committees. There is no reason why well-funded independent candidates cannot win races for the Legislature, municipal Mayor and eventually move into state and national offices.

Suggestion Five:
How about a non-party Party?
Communication, accountability, candidate training

Doesn't this all inevitably lead to the founding of a third political party in America? No, it certainly does not have to go in that direction at all. There is no need for a third political party, because honestly there is barely a legitimate reason for the two "major" parties we have today. The nation started without Democrats and Republicans. The two parties exist today because they have created a legal status for their organizations in state and federal laws. None of those laws can prohibit non-party members from participating in the process, raising money, recruiting and training candidates and running those candidates for office.

So why not start a non-party party? Why not start hundreds of them all across America. Call them people groups, networks, teams, guilds, associations or whatever you like. The legal mechanisms exist to accomplish all the necessary work that a party does without being a party. Is this just semantics? Hardly.

What if people started leaving political parties and became free agents? Here's a news flash: that is exactly what has been occurring for the past 20 years in amazing numbers. Take the battleground state of Ohio for example. You know the old line: No candidate can win the White House without winning Ohio? Well in Ohio that's a tougher task than ever for Republicans who make up about 13% of voter registration. Democrats only make up about 17%. About 68% of registered Ohio voters are non-aligned voters. They have no party at all.

This is the trend of the future in American politics. Americans are way too busy to bother with organizations that offer little in return. Political parties served limited purposes over history but they are virtually irrelevant to the voters of today. People don't need a blue ballot or a red ballot to find their way to the polls. They don't care about having a party slate card to tell them how to vote. They are certainly not heading to the community room to attend a candidates' night with ten people in attendance. They don't need bake sales, or a job working at the polls, they have the Internet, radio and cable news for their political information.

Political parties are a lot like statues in ancient churches. When people did not have the Bible to read, or could not read the Bible, the Gospel and church doctrine had to be communicated through liturgy and symbols. Once people were able to read the Scriptures, the need for more primitive forms of instruction were not as vital.

Back in the 1700's, Americans had no trouble reading for themselves. In fact literacy rates during the Jefferson administration were phenomenal. Parents, teachers, and local communities wanted everyone to be able to read the Bible for their personal welfare and

81

salvation, and they wanted all citizens familiar with the Declaration and the Constitution so that "religion and morality" would contribute to good citizenship. (See the Northwest Ordinance for more.)

The political problem was the lack of fast transmission of news and political debate. No Internet, high-speed cable, TV, radio, telephone, telegraph; no planes, cars, trains or steamships. Just newspapers published weekly at best and horses. This "need to know" created a niche for political busybodies and partisans. As the right to vote expanded past Congress and state legislatures to free citizens, the need to know increased all the more. Political parties formed as a human Internet to provide vital information to local voters. The parties used to be responsible for creating their own ballots. The county and state did the counting but the parties did the printing. So one Party would create a ballot list of their candidates on one color ballot paper. The opposing party would hand out a different color paper with their slate on the card. Voters would come to the polls and drop the colored cards into the ballot box.

We don't do that in America anymore for good reason. We don't wait for riders on horseback to bring us information from Washington D.C. We can all watch the US House and Senate in our homes and workplaces every moment they are in session, then hear about it on cable news and talk radio twenty four hours every day. Then there is the Internet. So exactly why do we need political parties in America today?

Just like honest newspapers publishers know the world is being changed by the Internet; honest politicos know the days of the current party system are numbered. They know somebody is going to write a book like this one. Some group, some where, is going to figure this all out and start a quiet revolution.

George Soros and the political left are already on the track and gaining speed. In 2004, Soros spent hundreds of millions on non-party affiliated activities that unquestionably impacted the Presidential election. His candidate lost, but Soros didn't quit. He went right back to building companies, non-profits, people networks, media shops and activist organizations to support his chosen candidates. George Soros is putting his money where his mouth is and it is not into traditional political parties.

Suggestion Six:
Get rid of contribution limits

There was an idea that looked good twenty years ago called campaign contributions. It turned out to be a bad idea. A bit of personal experience is in order here. In 1994, the Ohio Roundtable, a division of the American Policy Roundtable, led a citizen coalition to place contribution limits into Ohio election law. It seemed like the right thing to do, especially as a balancing point to enhance the value of term limits in state law. The citizen petition committee took two years to research and draft a law that was fully contained in just a few paragraphs on a single page of paper. The citizen petition was largely incorporated into a larger election reform measure and passed by the legislature.

It didn't take long for the politicians to find a way to beat the system. Truth be told, less than 24 hours after a final deal was made to accept the citizen reform measures, the Legislative leadership snuck an amendment into the measure and created a loophole. For years they worked to expand the loophole and create others so that today the Ohio limits are mostly ineffective.

Bottom line is this – politicians are going to find a way to beat every spending limit imagined by man. It's what they do and they will do it in such a way to create advantages for incumbents (themselves) and to discriminate against challengers. More importantly, creating contribution limits that do not contradict basic constitutional rights is a very tricky endeavor. The Supreme Court has rightly ruled spending money on political speech is free speech and should be protected.

The best way to solve this dilemma and create breathing space in the whole process is to abandon all contribution limits. Forget about it. Let any candidate take as much money from as many or as few people as they choose with one requirement. All contributions must be fully disclosed on the Internet within 24 hours of receipt or the money must be returned.

Let corporations give, unions give, everyone give. Since we now live in a full-information era – the very fact that a candidate may accept one million dollars from a major corporation or union will send a very clear message to every voter paying any attention at all.

"But big companies and unions will buy candidates and run them at will!" Which is exactly what is happening today. They just batch the smaller checks into one big pile and spread the money around so that no one can promptly trace it until the election is over.

Suggestion Seven:
Repeal McCain-Feingold and all its offspring

McCain Feingold is a federal law that severely restricts the rights of citizens to work in alliance with organizations and communicate about candidates and issues. It is a bad law that restricts free speech and protects incumbent politicians. It creates blackout periods just before the election where independent organizations cannot discuss a candidate's position on an issue. It is a dumb law and should be wiped off the books. If people want to spend their money to talk politics on the air, they should have the First Amendment right to do so. Wherever McCain-Feingold concepts have trickled into state politics (as in Florida law), all those restrictions should be removed as well.

Suggestion Eight:
Encourage the Opposition in Public Debate

Why are so many politicians afraid of free speech? Anyone participating in the public debate should encourage free exchange of ideas from all perspectives. Those who should be fighting the hardest for free political speech are those who care the most for religious liberty. It is no coincidence these two fundamental rights are discussed in the same amendment to the Constitution. Nor is it coincidental both rights are given first standing in the Bill of Rights, as "The First Amendment."

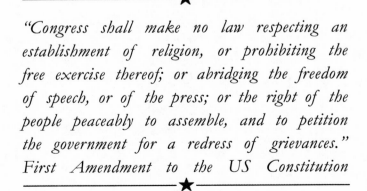

"Congress shall make no law respecting an establishment of religion, or prohibiting the free exercise thereof; or abridging the freedom of speech, or of the press; or the right of the people peaceably to assemble, and to petition the government for a redress of grievances." First Amendment to the US Constitution

Suggestion Nine:
Bury fear

Fear is a powerful motivational force. Some fear, as in the correct fear of the Lord, leads to wisdom. Some fear, as in the proper fear of electrocution can be a very positive quality, especially for an electrician. Unfounded fear can be a dangerous temptation that brings out the worst in fallen man. Fear is a very real temptation, especially to leaders.

In instances too numerous to mention, the Scriptures recount God sending a message to leaders to not be afraid. This kind of encounter happens so often because fighting fear must be a continual challenge for leaders.

Why would anyone advocating historic Constitutional principles be afraid to debate those ideas in America? Can there be stronger source documents or evidence than the Declaration, the Constitution, The Northwest Ordinance, the Articles of Confederation or the Federalist Papers? America was not built in a corner under a tarp to protect trade secrets. The ideas that make America unique have been heralded, debated, fought over and over for centuries. So why be afraid to present them in the current marketplace?

The principles behind those ideas also come from somewhere. The Founders claimed little originality. They leaned strongly on the Biblical teachings of the Reformation, the system of British Common Law flowing from the Magna Carta, and writers such as philosopher John Locke. History irrefutably proves the founding documents of America were built from the Judeo-Christian worldview of the West.

This point is especially imperative to Christians in the marketplace of ideas. Those who truly fear God can afford to fear little else. So often the spokespeople of evangelicalism speak on political matters in such strident, fearful tones. Some Christian leaders appear afraid to lose the political debate. Some seem fearful God will judge and condemn America if the wrong people are elected to public office or wrong issues are permitted to pass. They seem to have Sodom and Gomorrah on the mind. Those prophets may be doing a vital service to the nation. There is a God in heaven who sees injustice done on earth. The Bible teaches He retains the prerogative to judge mankind at will, but often delays His judgment in patient mercy. The fear is understandable but should be tempered by this reality for the Christian: no political tyrant or trend can change the historical reality of the resurrection of Jesus Christ. The Scriptures are clear: "All authority in heaven and earth has been given unto Me" (Matthew 28:18) says the risen Christ. Before Him "every knee shall bow and every tongue confess..." (Philippians 2:10) Thus the Christian comes to the debate not in fear of God's personal judgment, but in the hope of seeing mankind reconciled to God through the Gospel of Jesus Christ. By obeying the teachings of Jesus Christ civil societies avoid both the natural consequences of sinful behavior and the fear of judgment. In addition, building a civil society on laws anchored in the Judeo-Christian ethic provides the greatest liberty and benefits even for the total unbeliever.

Christians in the media are caught far too often trying to defend God, the Bible and the truth. Jesus said to Pontius Pilate: "Everyone on the side of truth listens to me." (John 18:37) The Christian is called to bear witness to the truth. It would be nice to win every shouting match on cable TV and talk radio, but that is not going to happen. Media hosts create controversy for ratings, not because they want to come to an honest conclusion in a logical debate. Modern Christians in the American debate have an additional advantage. When media critics accuse Christians of trying to "drive your personal morality down our throats," Christians can smile. The principles of the Declaration and the Constitution are not personal morality, they are historical realities based upon self-evident truth.

The best thing to do is simply hand a copy of the Declaration and the Constitution to the critics and ask them to reconcile their issue position with the principles of those two documents. What usually happens next is a rather embarrassing explosion where the critic begins to attack the Declaration and the Constitution as outdated documents of antiquity not worthy of modern consideration. At which point the debate has truly reached its logical conclusion. Some people still believe in America the way it was designed and has functioned for centuries. Some people don't.

It makes sense for Christians who understand the pain of sin to fear the consequences of bad behavior in civil society. St. Paul makes it clear, "the wages of sin is death." (Romans 6:23) This death involves the personal soul in eternity and the death of civility, common grace, and Liberty in culture. Modern history is replete with the disastrous consequences of totalitarian regimes that murdered millions in pursuit of a godless equation for national government. Godlessness in government is a scary reality that should cause any thinking person to be afraid.

In the 1940's, America responded to the fear of a world dominated by Adolph Hitler and the Axis powers. The Greatest Generation stared three brutal dictators in the eye, then paid the ultimate sacrifice of 450,00 lives to save America and the world from total disaster. Many historians believe if America had faced the fear sooner, far fewer lives would have been lost. The total death count in World War II was over 50 million people. There is real evil in the world. It is not to consume the faithful in fear. The answer to fear is best found in the words of St. Paul. The great herald of spiritual, personal and cultural liberty stated the antidote in these words: "Do not be overcome by evil, but overcome evil with good."

Suggestion Ten:
Invest in America

America is still the best deal on the market today. The Declaration and Constitution still exist. The current process of government is pretty messed up, but Americans have faced those kinds of challenges before.

America has two great assets that can be applied to meet this current challenge. The first is a generation of young people coming up who are ready for change. Some of them are liberals, even radicals today. Many of today's most conservative older leaders were once the flower children of the 60's. Life and truth have a way of bringing people to clearer perspectives.

There is a generation of kids coming up from private schools and home schools that are ready for positive change. Many of the greatest leaders in the Revolutionary Era were home schooled. The numbers of clear-thinking, well-educated young people coming online in America is a source of great potential. Yes, some are coming from public schools as well.

For all these kids to get an honest chance to fight for change, older Americans who have good jobs and have accumulated wealth are going to have to come to the table and open their checkbooks. Sam Adams and the Sons (and Daughters) of Liberty could not have prospered without the John Hancocks who gave up their resources for the future vision of America.

Older, prosperous Americans are going to have to make some serious financial commitments to keep the pathways open for this next generation. They will have to put up the money to fund organizations that will do the education and research, the legislative work, the candidate recruitment and training; and provide the communications tools and the radio, TV and Internet products to fuel this new army that is coming to the front.

It is essential for the grown-up generation to understand this critical point. These kids are an army ready to learn, grow and carry the torch of Liberty. But they cannot be left without resources. They cannot be treated the way Washington's Army was treated, left to bleed in the cold, underfed, underpaid, suffering from neglect from those they were dying to save. Investing in the next generation for Liberty must become a top priority.

The second great asset is technology. The ability to communicate historical, Biblical, philosophical and political information at light speed has never existed before. It is equally important that caring citizens embrace these new technologies and use them for the betterment of American culture. Investing in organizations that can utilize these technologies and investing in young leaders are both vitally important for America's future.

Chapter Ten
God Won't Be Voting this Year. Will You?

Now at last to the immediate crises, the short term problem: "Do I vote this year and how do I decide who to vote for?" Nothing in this chapter or this book is designed to try to directly influence the outcome of any specific electoral race for office. It's obvious this book is not written to lead anyone to a specific candidate or political party. The question is how do I decide?

The first step is to register to vote and make certain everyone in your circle of influence is registered to vote.

If you have moved since the last election, not voted in the past four year s, changed your name or address, please take the time to contact your local board of elections and re-register to vote. Just do it. You'll be glad you did.

Next, make sure you know the date of the next election.

Again, a quick call to the Board of Elections will tell you the date and the polling place where you go to vote in your neighborhood. Write it down on your calendar. Fix it in your daytimer or PDA. Place a note on the refrigerator. Set a plan on what time of day you will go to the polls. One of the biggest reasons people don't vote is that they forget.

Start finding places to get information on your candidates and ballot issues.

Pay attention to your local paper, especially the final thirty days before the election. Check the Internet for non-partisan sources. Look at the yard signs in your neighborhood and Google those names. Many candidates have websites that will give you a lot of information. Try USAVoter.com and VoteSmart.com - both are non-partisan sites.

Pay attention to ballot issues

If your state permits ballot issues for constitutional amendments and initiated statues, please get the facts and pay attention to these issues. They can have a huge impact on your life. So can local levies and tax issues. All these issues will appear in the newspapers in the month before the election.

Don't be afraid to ask questions.

You'll be surprised how many people care about elections and are going through exactly the same process. The back fence and front porch still work as communications tools.

How do I know the candidates are telling the truth?

You don't know. You might end up terribly disappointed. That's the risky part of the American system of government. It is based on the assumption people will tell the truth. Check their records on promises in the past. Ask "What has this person accomplished in the past that makes their promises credible today?" Think through the logic of their promise. Ask if they will have the power once in office to deliver or are they just giving you a line from their campaign playbook. When a Congressional or State Legislative candidate starts talking about issues, pay close attention. If they are not talking issues, ask them questions about important issues.

If they duck the question in public, follow up with a brief letter asking for a specific answer. Consider whether the candidate will be a member of the Majority or Minority of their legislative body. Members in the majority can deliver on promises. Minority party members may not have as much opportunity to introduce legislation that will reach a vote on the floor. If they are incumbents seeking re-election, ask them what they did in the past session regarding the issue of concern. They will figure out quickly you know enough about their world to either give you a straight answer or head for the exit door.

When it comes to Presidential candidates another important grid has to be added. Remember, the President is the Chief Executive of the Government and the Commander-in-Chief. When it comes to foreign policy the President has a defining constitutional power. The same is true for appointments to the Federal Judiciary, including the Supreme Court. The President can't do it all without the Congress, but in these areas the Constitution gives the President a pathway to leadership.

That being said, when the question is the federal budget, healthcare, abortion, global warming, embryonic stem cell research, school choice, educational testing or a myriad of issues, the President can't get it done without the Congress. So when candidates for the White House come along and start talking issues straight out of their campaign playbook start asking this question out loud; "Will he/she have the votes in Congress to get that done?"

Don't get caught believing the playbook sound bites if the votes are not there in the Congress. If the Candidate is a Democrat and will have the backing of a Democrat majority in Congress then promises may be possible – no guarantees – but possible. If the

Candidate is Republican with a Republican majority in Congress the same is true. But if the government in Washington D.C. is divided, then most campaign promises are shaky and could be just rhetoric from the playbook designed to win votes on Election Day.

How to deal with the ballot on Election Day
1) Don't overvalue the races at the top

Don't be convinced that the race for the Presidency, Governor or Senator is necessarily the most important vote you will cast. Every year races for local mayor, state representative and ballot issues are decided by a handful of votes. Your vote may be the one that actually makes all the difference in an election farther down the ballot. The Presidency is important but so are the races for US Congress and State Legislature. Don't forget these people make more decisions about your life than the President ever will. Remember the balance of three branches of government. Vote balanced.

2) Decide the issues that are most important to you. List them in order of priority.

Let your conscience be your guide. Forget political parties. Forget the slick TV commercials. Create a list that ranks the issues you care most about and then match the candidates to your issues. Chances are very good you will be disappointed that none of the candidates for the White House measure up exactly to your grid. Hopefully one will emerge that is better than the rest.

3) Dare I choose between candidates that are far below my expectations?

You don't have to vote the race for the Presidency. You can

vote the rest of the ballot and skip any race you chose. Think this through carefully. One of the names on the ballot will win the race. One of them will become President of the United States. Which one will likely do more harm to the nation? Which one will likely do less harm? Think about what is best for preserving the common good of the nation. Vote strategically.

Please remember you are not voting for a king to rule over you. You are casting your ballot as a shareholder toward the hiring of the Chief Executive for a period of 48 months. You can vote to throw the bum out in four years if necessary. You also are voting for members of Congress who have the power to counter-balance the President, so treat those races with equal care.

For the many culture warriors on all sides of the struggle who consider the race for the Presidency to be the ultimate defining moment, please try this on for size. There will be another election in 208 weeks. A single election is significant, but in America, it is not the end or the beginning of the world. Those defining moments happen around the dinner table, in the local church and synagogue, in schools and town halls and across the spectrum of media every single day. Take a historical breath.

Voting is sometimes like a chess match or playing scrabble. On occasion you have to make a move or cast a vote you don't like very much, but it stops something worse from happening. Of course that is most undesirable; but it can also be the most responsible action at the time.

Can you cast a protest vote? Of course you can vote for whomever you wish. You can vote for a totally unknown person running for President to deny others your vote. You can use your vote to make a statement and build support for an unknown new party. You can write in any name you wish as a pure protest as well. The write-in vote may not count, but it might make you feel better. Your vote is your voice. You have the right to use it as you wish, but remember, your vote is also a sacred responsibility you inherited. Someone else paid the price so that you could have the right to vote.

Hate voting for the lesser of two evils? Who doesn't? Maybe it's time to change the language here. As has already been illustrated, there are no perfect candidates so the choice will always be between imperfect, fallen candidates. The best way to solve this problem is to implement the suggestions found in chapter seven. You can work with others on the long term solutions every day for the next four years. On Election Day, we the people must do the choosing based on the ballot before us. If you don't vote, someone else will make the decisions for you. Do your part and then use your energy to fight the bigger issues so that the choices are better in four years. Don't walk out of the polling place saying "thank God that's over." Walk out and call somebody to start working on the next election immediately.

A final note: living in a governmental system where the consent of the governed is honored is one of the greatest of all gifts. We can never accurately quantify the cost of securing this right. Nor can we imagine the darkness that would descend upon America if this right is lost. Every time we participate in the electoral process we remind every incumbent politician, every member of the media and every nation in the watching world that the founding American ideals are still alive.

In every election cycle the questions of religious faith will arise. It has always been that way in America and it only makes sense. Given the words of the Declaration this should come as no surprise.

Some people will try to default to God in this election cycle. They will claim the candidates are not worthy of the votes of the faithful. They will claim voting is irrelevant because God appoints leaders. They will accuse those who chose between "the lesser of two evils" are somehow abandoning a Biblical ethic. Some will even hide behind piety and claim voting is worldly and good Christians don't get involved in worldly affairs. All these shirk a responsibility clearly delegated to man by the God of the Bible.

Hopefully, everyone casting a ballot on Election Day will do so prayerfully. Voting is a sacred trust and calls for Divine wisdom. One thing is certain from a Biblical and historical perspective, God will not be voting this year. He delegated that job to us, if we have the courage to embrace this responsibility.

Appendix
How the Electoral College Works
Melanie Elsey
National Legislative Director
The American Policy Roundtable

The unique system of selecting the President of the United States is outlined in Article II, section 1 of the US Constitution and improved twice through the XII and XXIII amendments. The executive power of the most powerful nation on earth is vested in this office and it was the intent of the Founding Fathers that the President would be independently chosen in a process distinct from the selection of the members of Congress.

According to a report prepared by the Congressional Research Service (order code RS20273, 9/8/2003), "The Constitutional Convention of 1787 considered several methods of electing the President, including selection by Congress, by the governors of the states, by the state legislatures, by a special group of Members of Congress chosen by lot and by direct popular election. Late in the convention, the matter was referred to the Committee of eleven on Postponed Matters, which devised the Electoral College system in its original form. This plan, which met with widespread approval by the delegates, was incorporated into the document with only minor changes."

The Electoral College system was described by Alexander

Hamilton, "...if the manner of it be not perfect, it is at least excellent. It unites in an eminent degree all the advantages, the union of which was to be wished for." (Federalist Paper No. 68, 3/14/1788) These advantages include the separation of state and federal interests, providing critical leverage to less populous states, and the insulation of the election of the President from political manipulation. (CRS, 9/8/2003)

"They have not made the appointment of the President to depend on any preexisting bodies of men, who might be tampered with beforehand to prostitute their votes; but they have referred it in the first instance to an immediate act of the people of America, to be exerted in the choice of persons for the temporary and sole purpose of making the appointment." (Fed. Paper No. 68)

The Constitution requires that each state have a number of "electors" equal to its combined representation in the US Senate and US House of Representatives. In each state these electors are to be chosen in a manner directed by the state legislature. In the earliest years of the republic most state legislators chose to directly select the electors. However, state laws changed in the early 1800's to provide selection by popular vote, which remains the system in use today. Since the membership of the US House of Representatives is determined in number by census data collected every ten years, the Electoral College for 2004 and 2008 has a total of 538 members – reflecting 100 US Senators, 435 US Representatives, and 3 representing Washington DC. The Constitution also requires that the President must receive a majority of the electoral vote, which currently stands at 270.

After the general citizenry votes for President and Vice-President in November, the electors convene in their respective states on a day determined by Congress. The electors (chosen in most states by Party Conventions) have their vote to the candidate represented by the popular vote.

What does this look like?

If the Democratic candidates for President and Vice President win the popular vote, then the pre-selected electors for that slate of candidates will meet to cast their electoral votes on behalf of the entire state. If the Republican candidates for President and Vice President win the popular vote, then the pre-selected electors (a different group than the Democratic electors) for that slate of candidates will meet to cast their electoral votes on behalf of the entire state. In all but two states, it is a winner-take-all method. Only Maine and Nebraska currently have the potential to split their electoral votes, which to date has never happened.

Once the votes are cast in state central locations (usually state capitals), the results are certified, sealed, and sent to the Vice-President. The Electoral College votes are officially counted in a joint session of Congress on January 6th of the subsequent year. A majority of Electoral College votes are required to elect the President. Congress is constitutionally obligated to recognize the vote of the limited number of electors for each state, not the aggregate total of popular votes. If a majority of Electoral College votes are not achieved by any candidate, the decision shifts to the US House of Representatives for the Presidential election and to the US Senate for the Vice-Presidential election.

Distribution of 2004 and 2008 Electoral Votes

State	2004 and 2008		
Alabama	9	Montana	3
Alaska	3	Nebraska	5
Arizona	10	Nevada	5
Arkansas	6	New Hampshire	4
California	55	New Jersey	15
Colorado	9	New Mexico	5
Connecticut	7	New York	31
Delaware	3	North Carolina	15
D.C.	3	North Dakota	3
Florida	27	Ohio	20
Georgia	15	Oklahoma	7
Hawaii	4	Oregon	7
Idaho	4	Pennsylvania	21
Illinois	21	Rhode Island	4
Indiana	11	South Carolina	8
Iowa	7	South Dakota	3
Kansas	6	Tennessee	11
Kentucky	8	Texas	34
Louisiana	9	Utah	5
Maine	4	Vermont	3
Maryland	10	Virginia	13
Massachusetts	12	Washington	11
Michigan	17	West Virginia	5
Minnesota	10	Wisconsin	10
Mississippi	6	Wyoming	3
Missouri	11		

Source: US National Archives and Records Administration. These allocations are based on the 2000 Census. Total number of electoral votes= 538; majority needed to elect the President = 270

Frequently Asked Questions:

Q. How are the electors selected to represent the Electoral College for each state?

A. This is determined by state legislatures and varies from state to state. The state party conventions are used as the selection process in 34 states. In 10 states the selections are made by the state central committee.

Q. Is it possible for an elector to the state's Electoral College to cast their vote for a candidate who did not secure the majority popular vote?

A. It depends on state law. In some states it would be possible for an Electoral College delegate to act as a "faithless elector" and not stand by the commitment to vote for the candidate which won the popular vote. There is no constitutional requirement to vote for the candidate they represent. This has occurred in a handful of circumstances, but has never affected the outcome of an election.

Q. What are the advantages to using the Electoral College system of electing the US President?

A. Primarily, it preserves the influence of the citizenry in the smaller states. There are seven states in addition to Washington DC that have 3 Electoral College votes. The largest state is California, with 55 Electoral College votes. Under this system, especially in a close election, it is particularly important for candidates to market their policies and philosophical positions to even the smallest states.

Q. Did the Founding Fathers give consideration to a straight popular vote for the US President?

A. This approach was specifically rejected by the Founders at the Constitutional Convention. If it were the method used today, candidates would be focusing on the more populous areas, such as the large urban centers and would have very little incentive to secure the vote.

About the Author

David Zanotti prefers to be introduced as the grandson of Italian immigrants, a nobody from nowhere in particular. A kid raised in a family of six in a small home by parents of the WWII generation. He considers himself a debtor to all who gave him the privilege of being born and raised in America.

He was elected class president in the 8th grade at Holy Family School because his fellow students thought he could speak well in public. Not long after, he was in trouble with the principal for doing comic impersonations of the school faculty. He was elected to student council and served as Vice-President at Valley Forge High School in the early 1970's. As a student activist, he protested the war in Viet Nam and helped bring Dennis Kucinich to his high school as a special speaker, at a program called Rap Week. Fortunately no photos or audio tapes have survived.

Mr. Zanotti's first visit to a statehouse and first political campaign work began as a college student in 1978. He attended Cuyahoga Community College, Mt. Vernon Nazarene College, and did graduate work at Ashland University. He left the world of manufacturing in 1985 to join the Roundtable.

Today David Zanotti serves as President/CEO of the American Policy Roundtable, a non-profit, non-partisan, independent public policy organization founded in 1980. He also serves as President of Roundtable Freedom Forum, a legislative organization and is

Chairman of The Liberty Committee, a federal Political Action Committee.

The Roundtable works everyday to tell the story of American liberty and the founding principles upon which it stands. Over the years the Roundtable has built a network of citizen support in several battle ground states including Ohio, Florida, Pennsylvania, West Virginia, and Tennessee.

The Roundtable and Freedom Forum have helped citizens overcome a number of challenges by providing positive alternatives in public policy. The Roundtable has effectively led numerous ballot issue campaigns and assisted in the passage and defeat of legislation. From the local school board to the US Supreme Court, the Roundtable has participated in several reform efforts in education policy, including the landmark US Supreme Court decision on school choice. Roundtable and Freedom Forum alliances have also helped defeat several initiatives including the expansion of casino gambling and the federal takeover of health care. For a timeline of Roundtable projects and accomplishments please visit APRoundtable.org.

In 1989, Roundtable began a daily news and commentary broadcast titled, The Public Square®, which is one of the longest running daily radio broadcasts in America. Mr. Zanotti has hosted The Public Square® from its first broadcast. Today, The Public Square®, co-hosted with Wayne Shepherd, is heard daily in eight states and across the nation via the Internet and on special national broadcasts. In October 2007, The Public Square® hosted the national radio special, "The God Delusion Debate" on the Moody Radio Network and Salem Radio.

Mr. Zanotti and the work of the Roundtable have appeared

105

on ABC News, NBC News, CBS News, PBS Frontline, The McNeil/Lehrer Report, Fox News, MSNBC, CNN, CNBC, C-SPAN, National Public Radio, The National Press Club, The Wall Street Journal, USAToday, The Washington Post, The Washington Times, The New York Times, The Chicago Tribune, The Dallas Daily News, The LA Times, The San Francisco Chronicle, Time, Newsweek, US News and World Report, the BBC and several foreign media services. He also bumped into Larry King at a coffee shop in Beverly Hills, but has yet to make an appearance on Larry King Live.

Mr. Zanotti has been blessed in marriage to the same wonderful wife since 1976. Together, they have worked to raise three children in the hope of faith, family and liberty. His favorite movies are all comedies. He would still rather have lunch with Billy Crystal or Bill Cosby than attend a meeting in the White House or on Capitol Hill.

Why I am Not a Values Voter©

By David Zanotti
President/CEO
The American Policy Roundtable
Founded 1980

In 2004, a carefully crafted strategy came forward from a group of Christian leaders meeting in Washington D.C. who launched the term "values voter." They have marketed this label effectively, creating a new stereotype the media now uses to define people of faith who participate in the political process. I personally respect the rights of these leaders and appreciate their effort to participate in the voting process. I do not, however, subscribe to their terminology or "movement" for the following reasons:

1) The "values voter" strategy is following the traditional pattern of special interest politics. The circle being drawn by the leaders of this movement excludes far too much historical reality. The Biblical worldview is not a minority position in American culture nor should it be treated as such. America's founding is based largely on Biblical principles. Attempting to "circle-up" Bible-believing people and use their numbers for political leverage is a short-sighted strategy. The appeal should be for all Americans to carefully consider these founding principles and to re-align our government accordingly.

2) Values are transitory. The term became popular in educational circles during the 1970's, back in the days of the Silent Majority and just before the rise of the Moral Majority. Anyone can define values based on their individual liking. George Soros and the radical left have values too, just different values.

3) Branding all people of faith as "values voters" is too confining. Most people prefer to make their own political decisions. Getting stereotyped into a movement based on the decisions of a private group meeting in Washington, D.C. doesn't sit well with most people.

4) So far the track record of "values voters" leaders is exclusively Republican. The leaders are clearly trying to align churches and religious leaders to the Republican Party. I have nothing against the Republican Party and recognize its right to legally exist. I just can't figure out why "values voters" want to market their message to only one-third of the voting population. Last time I checked you still need 50.1% to win most elections and much higher margins to win legislative and ballot issues. It's tough to get pumped up about a strategy that only gets you one-third of the way toward the finish line.

The Declaration, the Constitution, and the principles on which they stand are bigger than all of this. We pray for the leaders of this movement regularly and certainly wish them no ill. To solve America's bigger problems, however, we have to start drawing bigger circles.

What the Heck is a PAC Anyways?

We hear about them all the time. Most of the media coverage on PAC's is shaded toward the negative.

A PAC is a Political Action Committee. A PAC is an organization created by filing a form with the Federal Elections Commission and/or a state elections commission or agency such as the Secretary of State's office. The paperwork is relatively simple to file and reporting not terribly complicated.

The purpose of a PAC is to permit individuals to join together in channeling political contributions to specific candidates. This notion began in the post-Watergate era as part of a reform movement at the Federal level. Eventually the states began to follow in form. PACs are supposed to give everyone a chance to see the reporting processes on how candidate campaigns raise and spend money.

Some PAC's do more than simply gather funds for endorsed candidates. Some raise money, hire staff and work to recruit and train candidates. In essence, a PAC is a way for individual citizens and networks of interested citizens to unite and attempt to legally impact the outcome of elections. You'd think people could do that without filing a bunch of paperwork in a free nation like America. Politicians don't like the idea of competition or free agents out there so they force this method of participation and reporting. Fortunately, the Constitution and the Courts have kept politicians from getting even more aggressive in limiting citizen participation.

Is it a good idea be involved with or contributing to a PAC?

If you find a PAC that aligns with your core principles and knows how to effectively work with candidates, it might be a very good idea. PAC contributions and contributions to candidate campaigns are not tax deductible per IRS regulations but are still very important.

The Declaration of Independence

IN CONGRESS, JULY 4, 1776

The unanimous Declaration of the thirteen united States of America

When in the Course of human events it becomes necessary for one people to dissolve the political bands which have connected them with another and to assume among the powers of the earth, the separate and equal station to which the Laws of Nature and of Nature's God entitle them, a decent respect to the opinions of mankind requires that they should declare the causes which impel them to the separation.

We hold these truths to be self-evident, that all men are created equal, that they are endowed by their Creator with certain unalienable Rights, that among these are Life, Liberty and the pursuit of Happiness. — That to secure these rights, Governments are instituted among Men, deriving their just powers from the consent of the governed, — That whenever any Form of Government becomes destructive of these ends, it is the Right of the People to alter or to abolish it, and to institute new Government, laying its foundation on such principles and organizing its powers in such form, as to them shall seem most likely to effect their Safety and Happiness. Prudence, indeed, will dictate that Governments long established should not be changed for light and transient causes; and accordingly all experience hath shewn that mankind are more disposed to suffer, while evils are sufferable than to right themselves by abolishing the forms to which they are accustomed. But when a long train of abuses and usurpations, pursuing invariably the same Object evinces a design to reduce them under absolute Despotism, it is their right, it is their duty, to throw off such Government, and to provide new Guards for their future security. — Such has been the patient sufferance of these Colonies; and such is now the necessity which constrains them to alter their former Systems of Government. The history of the present King of Great Britain is a history of repeated injuries and usurpations, all having in direct object the establishment of an absolute Tyranny over these States. To prove this, let Facts be submitted to a candid world.

He has refused his Assent to Laws, the most wholesome and necessary for the public good.

He has forbidden his Governors to pass Laws of immediate and pressing importance, unless suspended in their operation till his Assent should be obtained; and when so suspended, he has utterly neglected to attend to them.

He has refused to pass other Laws for the accommodation of large districts of people, unless those people would relinquish the right of Representation in the Legislature, a right inestimable to them and formidable to tyrants only.

He has called together legislative bodies at places unusual, uncomfortable, and distant from the depository of their Public Records, for the sole purpose of fatiguing them into compliance with his measures.

He has dissolved Representative Houses repeatedly, for opposing with manly firmness his invasions on the rights of the people.

He has refused for a long time, after such dissolutions, to cause others to be elected, whereby the Legislative Powers, incapable of Annihilation, have returned to the People at large for their exercise; the State remaining in the mean time exposed to all the dangers of invasion from without, and convulsions within.

He has endeavoured to prevent the population of these States; for that purpose obstructing the Laws for Naturalization of Foreigners; refusing to pass others to encourage their migrations hither, and raising the conditions of new Appropriations of Lands.

He has obstructed the Administration of Justice by refusing his Assent to Laws for establishing Judiciary Powers.

He has made Judges dependent on his Will alone for the tenure of their offices, and the amount and payment of their salaries.

He has erected a multitude of New Offices, and sent hither swarms of Officers to harass our people and eat out their substance.

He has kept among us, in times of peace, Standing Armies without the Consent of our legislatures.

He has affected to render the Military independent of and superior to the Civil Power.

He has combined with others to subject us to a jurisdiction foreign to our constitution, and unacknowledged by our laws; giving his Assent to their Acts of pretended Legislation:

For quartering large bodies of armed troops among us:

For protecting them, by a mock Trial from punishment for any Murders which they should commit on the Inhabitants of these States:

For cutting off our Trade with all parts of the world:

For imposing Taxes on us without our Consent:

For depriving us in many cases, of the benefit of Trial by Jury:

For transporting us beyond Seas to be tried for pretended offences:

For abolishing the free System of English Laws in a neighbouring Province, establishing therein an Arbitrary government, and enlarging its Boundaries so as to render it at once an example and fit instrument for introducing the same absolute rule into these Colonies

For taking away our Charters, abolishing our most valuable Laws and altering fundamentally the Forms of our Governments:

For suspending our own Legislatures, and declaring themselves invested with power to legislate for us in all cases whatsoever.

He has abdicated Government here, by declaring us out of his Protection and waging War against us.

He has plundered our seas, ravaged our coasts, burnt our towns, and destroyed the lives of our people.

He is at this time transporting large Armies of foreign Mercenaries to compleat the works of death, desolation, and tyranny, already begun with circumstances of Cruelty & Perfidy scarcely paralleled in the most barbarous ages, and totally unworthy the Head of a civilized nation.

He has constrained our fellow Citizens taken Captive on the high Seas to bear Arms against their Country, to become the executioners of their friends and Brethren, or to fall themselves by their Hands.

He has excited domestic insurrections amongst us, and has endeavoured to bring on the inhabitants of our frontiers, the merciless Indian Savages whose known rule of warfare, is an undistinguished destruction of all ages, sexes and conditions.

In every stage of these Oppressions We have Petitioned for Redress in the most humble terms: Our repeated Petitions have been answered only by repeated injury. A Prince, whose character is thus marked by every act which may define a Tyrant, is unfit to be the ruler of a free people.

Nor have We been wanting in attentions to our British brethren. We have warned them from time to time of attempts by their legislature to extend an unwarrantable jurisdiction over us. We have reminded them of the circumstances of our emigration and settlement here. We have appealed to their native justice and magnanimity, and we have conjured them by the ties of our common kindred to disavow these usurpations, which would inevitably interrupt our connections and correspondence. They too have been deaf to the voice of justice and of consanguinity. We must, therefore, acquiesce in the necessity, which denounces our Separation, and hold them, as we hold the rest of mankind, Enemies in War, in Peace Friends.

We, therefore, the Representatives of the united States of America, in General Congress, Assembled, appealing to the Supreme Judge of the world for the rectitude of our intentions, do, in the Name, and by Authority of the good People of these Colonies, solemnly publish and declare, That these united Colonies are, and of Right ought to be Free and Independent States, that they are Absolved from all Allegiance to the British Crown, and that all political connection between them and the State of Great Britain, is and ought to be totally dissolved; and that as Free and Independent States, they have full Power to levy War, conclude Peace, contract Alliances, establish Commerce, and to do all other Acts and Things which Independent States may of right do. — And for the support of this Declaration, with a firm reliance on the protection of Divine Providence, we mutually pledge to each other our Lives, our Fortunes, and our sacred Honor.

Suggested Reading

The Declaration of Independence

http://www.archives.gov/national-archives-experience/charters/declaration.html

The US Constitution

http://www.law.cornell.edu/constitution/constitution.overview.html

The Northwest Ordinance

http://usinfo.state.gov/usa/infousa/facts/democrac/5.htm

The Federalist Papers

http://thomas.loc.gov/home/histdox/fedpapers.html

Johnson, Paul M., "History of the American People," *Harper Perennial*, February 1999

Amos, Gary T., "Defending the Declaration," *Providence Foundation*, August 1996

Eidsmoe, John, "Christianity and the Constitution," *Baker Academic*, August 1995

Printed in the United States
200772BV00002B/1-66/A